The survey kit

DATE DUE

ILL R18 1434676			
11·24·01			
NOV 2 5 2001			

THE SURVEY KIT

Purpose: The purposes of this 9-volume Kit are to enable readers to prepare and conduct surveys and become better users of survey results. Surveys are conducted to collect information by asking questions of people on the telephone, face-to-face, and by mail. The questions can be about attitudes, beliefs, and behavior as well as socioeconomic and health status. To do a good survey also means knowing how to ask questions, design the survey (research) project, sample respondents, collect reliable and valid information, and analyze and report the results. You also need to know how to plan and budget for your survey.

Users: The Kit is for students in undergraduate and graduate classes in the social and health sciences and for individuals in the public and private sectors who are responsible for conducting and using surveys. Its primary goal is to enable users to prepare surveys and collect data that are accurate and useful for primarily practical purposes. Sometimes, these practical purposes overlap the objectives of scientific research, and so survey researchers will also find the Kit useful.

Format of the Kit: All books in the series contain instructional objectives, exercises and answers, examples of surveys in use and illustrations of survey questions, guidelines for action, checklists of do's and don'ts, and annotated references.

Volumes in The Survey Kit:

1. **The Survey Handbook**
   Arlene Fink

2. **How to Ask Survey Questions**
   Arlene Fink

3. **How to Conduct Self-Administered and Mail Surveys**
   Linda B. Bourque and *Eve P. Fielder*

4. **How to Conduct Interviews by Telephone and in Person**
   James H. Frey and *Sabine Mertens Oishi*

5. **How to Design Surveys**
   Arlene Fink

6. **How to Sample in Surveys**
   Arlene Fink

7. **How to Measure Survey Reliability and Validity**
   Mark S. Litwin

8. **How to Analyze Survey Data**
   Arlene Fink

9. **How to Report on Surveys**
   Arlene Fink

THE SURVEY KIT 1

THE SURVEY
HANDBOOK

ARLENE FINK

SAGE Publications
International Educational and Professional Publisher
Thousand Oaks   London   New Delhi

For information address:

 SAGE Publications, Inc.
2455 Teller Road
Thousand Oaks, California 91320
E-mail: order@sagepub.com

SAGE Publications Ltd.
6 Bonhill Street
London EC2A 4PU
United Kingdom

SAGE Publications India Pvt. Ltd.
M-32 Market
Greater Kailash I
New Delhi 110 048 India

Printed in the United States of America

Library of Congress Cataloging-in-Publication Data

Main entry under title:

The survey kit.
    p. cm.
    Includes bibliographical references.
    Contents: v. 1. The survey handbook / Arlene Fink — v. 2. How to ask survey questions / Arlene Fink — v. 3. How to conduct self-administered and mail surveys / Linda B. Bourque, Eve P. Fielder — v. 4. How to conduct interviews by telephone and in person / James H. Frey, Sabine Mertens Oishi — v. 5. How to design surveys / Arlene Fink — v. 6. How to sample in surveys / Arlene Fink — v. 7. How to measure survey reliability and validity / Mark S. Litwin — v. 8. How to analyze survey data / Arlene Fink — v. 9. How to report on surveys / Arlene Fink.
    ISBN 0-8039-7388-8 (pbk. : The survey kit : alk. paper)
    1. Social surveys. 2. Health surveys. I. Fink, Arlene.
HN29.S724   1995
300′.723—dc20   95-12712

This book is printed on acid-free paper.

99 10 9 8 7 6

Sage Production Editor: Diane S. Foster
Sage Copy Editor: Joyce Kuhn
Sage Typesetter: Janelle LeMaster

Contents

The Survey Handbook: Learning Objectives

The major goal of this handbook is to introduce you to the skills and resources you need to conduct a survey. The skills include identifying specific survey objectives, designing studies and sampling respondents, developing reliable and valid self-administered questionnaires and interviews, administering the survey, and analyzing and reporting the results. The handbook also aims to teach you how to organize surveys and estimate their costs and contains examples of management plans the budgets.

The specific objectives are:

- Identify the characteristics of high-quality surveys

- Describe the usefulness in surveys of specific objectives, straightforward questions, sound research design, sound choice of population or sample, reliable and valid instruments, appropriate analysis, accurate reporting of results, and reasonable resources

- Distinguish between four types of survey instruments

- Define reliability and its characteristics

- Define validity and its characteristics

- Interpret data from open-ended questions using the "liked best / liked least" method

- Distinguish between the uses of figures and tables in survey results

- Describe the activities that constitute a "typical" survey

- List the questions to ask in pilot tests

- Relate survey costs to needs for personnel and time for the survey

- Understand the relationships between time, scope, and quality in survey design and implementation

- Understand the contents and characteristics of survey budget presentations

1 What Is a Survey? When Do You Use One?

A survey is a system for collecting information to describe, compare, or explain knowledge, attitudes, and behavior. Surveys involve setting objectives for information collection, designing research, preparing a reliable and valid data collection instrument, administering and scoring the instrument, analyzing data, and reporting the results.

Surveys are taken of political and consumer choices, use of health services, numbers of people in the labor force, and opinions on just about everything from aardvarks to zyzyvas. Individuals, communities, schools, businesses, and researchers use surveys to find out about people by asking questions about feelings, motivations, plans, beliefs, and personal backgrounds. The questions in survey instruments are typically

1

arranged into mailed, taped, or self-administered questionnaires (on paper or on a computer) and into in-person (face-
to-face) or telephone interviews.

Surveys are a prominent part of life in many major indus-
trialized nations, particularly the United States. The absurdity
of some survey questions are symbolized in the following
cartoon.

Drawing by R. Chast published in the February 10, 1986 issue of *The New
Yorker* (p. 43). © 1986 by The New Yorker Magazine, Inc. Reprinted by
permission.

U.S. elections are always accompanied by a flood of polls. Polling is a major type of survey but far from the only kind. Other types of surveys are now widely used in conjunction with a variety of projects and activities. As Example 1.1 shows, surveys are used in very diverse settings, such as deciding on the perfect painting and making public policy regarding the environment.

EXAMPLE 1.1
Art and Sea Otters: Two Surveys

Survey on Art

What would a genuine people's art look like? Can artists make paintings that truly reflect the tastes of the American public? To find out, two artists conducted a phone survey of 1,001 adults. The following are some of the questions they asked:

- Do you prefer pictures from a long time ago, like Lincoln or Jesus?
- Which do you think you like better, a painting of one person or a painting of a group of people?
- Would you rather see paintings of outdoor scenes or indoor scenes?
- If you had to name one color as your favorite, what would it be?
- Would you say you prefer paintings in which the person or people are nude, partially clothed, or fully clothed?

(Excerpts from "The Perfect Painting," by Richard B. Woodward in February 20, 1994 issue of the *New York Times Magazine,* pp. 36-37. Copyright © 1994 by the New York Times Company. Reprinted by permission.)

Survey on Sea Otters

How much is a Pacific sea otter's life worth—not as someone's pet but as a wild animal that will never be studied by scientists or frolic in front of tourists? Could the U.S. government find out how much they would voluntarily pay to keep the otter safe from unnatural hazards?

Until recently, such abstract questions have mostly been grist for academic debate. But now federal regulators are under orders from Congress and the courts to figure ways to measure losses to people not directly affected by environmental problems like oil spills or haze in national parks. The first set of guidelines, from the National Oceanic and Atmospheric Administration, is due later this month [September 1993] and is widely expected to support the use of survey-based techniques.

_____

(Excerpts from "Economic Watch; Disputed New Role for Polls: Putting a Price Tag on Nature," by Peter Passell in September 6, 1993 issue of the *New York Times*, p. A1. Copyright © 1993 by the New York Times Company. Reprinted by permission.)

A surveyor's job can be very rewarding in its variety and in intellectual challenges. What does the typical survey expert need to know? One way to answer the question is to consider the requirements for getting a job as a surveyor.

Example 1.2 is an excerpt from a typical advertisement for an employment opportunity that might appear in the classified advertisement section of a newspaper.

EXAMPLE 1.2
A Job in a Survey Center

Project Coordinator

Assisting the department director in carrying out applied survey research, your duties will include: formulating study designs and sampling frames; . . . developing instruments; supervising data collection, entry, and manipulation; application of descriptive and inferential statistics; interpreting results and preparing reports.

The "duties" specified in the advertisement are typical skills required to conduct surveys. This book introduces all of them: study design and sampling; survey instrument development, with emphasis on asking straightforward questions and developing reliable and valid instruments (including in-person and telephone interviews and self-administered questionnaires); data collection and statistical analysis and interpretation; and report preparation. The book also discusses how to plan surveys and prepare a budget for them.

The best surveys have these features:

- Specific objectives
- Straightforward questions
- Sound research design
- Sound choice of population or sample
- Reliable and valid survey instruments
- Appropriate analysis
- Accurate reporting of survey results
- Reasonable resources

Survey Objectives:
Measuring Hoped-For Outcomes

What should the survey ask? What information should it collect? You must know the survey's objectives to answer these questions. An objective is a statement of the survey's hoped-for outcomes. Example 1.3 contains three objectives for a survey of educational needs.

EXAMPLE 1.3
Illustrative Objectives for a
Survey of Educational Needs

1. Identify the most common needs for educational services
2. Compare needs of men and women
3. Determine the characteristics of people who benefit most from services

---

A specific set of objectives like these suggests a survey that asks questions about the following:

Objective 1: Educational needs

Sample survey question: Which of the following skills would you like to have?

Objective 2: Gender

Sample survey question: Are you male or female?

Objective 3, first part: Characteristics of survey participants

Sample survey questions: What is your occupation? What was your household income last year? How much television do you watch? How many books do you read in an average month?

Objective 3, second part: Benefits

Sample survey question: To what extent has this program helped you improve your job skills? (In this example, you can infer that one benefit is improvement in job skills.)

Suppose you add these objectives:

EXAMPLE 1.4
More Objectives for a
Survey of Educational Needs

4. Compare younger and older parents in their needs for education in managing a household and caring for a child

5. Determine the relationship between parents' education and method of disciplining children for mild, moderate, and severe infractions

---

If you add objectives to the survey, you may need to add questions to the instrument. To collect information for the new objectives, for example, you need to ask about the following:

- Parents' age
- How parents manage their household
- How parents care for their children

- Level of parents' education
- Methods for disciplining children for mild, moderate, and severe infractions

When planning a survey and its instrument, define all potentially imprecise or ambiguous terms in the objectives. For the objectives above, the imprecise terms are needs; educational services; characteristics; benefit; younger and older; household management; child care; discipline methods; and mild, moderate, and severe infractions. Why are these terms ambiguous? No standard definition exists for any of them. What are needs, for example, and of the very long list that you might create, which are so important that they should be included on the survey? What is discipline? In a later section, this chapter discusses how focus groups and consensus panels can be used to determine a survey's objectives and help define and clarify their meaning.

Survey objectives can also be converted into questions or hypotheses to be researched by a change in sentence structure, as illustrated in Example 1.5 with Survey Objectives 4 and 5 listed earlier (Example 1.4).

EXAMPLE 1.5
Survey Objectives, Research Questions, and Hypotheses

Survey Objective 4

To compare younger and older parents in their needs to learn how to manage a household and care for a child

Survey Research Question: How do younger and older parents compare in their needs to learn how to manage a household and care for a child?

Research Hypothesis: No differences exist between younger and older parents in their needs to learn how to manage a household and care for a child.

Survey Objective 5

To determine the relationship between parents' education and method of disciplining children for mild, moderate, and severe infractions

Survey Research Question: What is the relationship between parents' education and method of disciplining children for mild, moderate, and severe infractions?

Research Hypothesis: No relationship exists between parents' education and method of disciplining children for mild, moderate, and severe infractions.

If you achieve Survey Objective 4 or answer its associated question or properly test its associated hypothesis, you will provide data on younger and older parents' needs to learn to manage a household and care for a child. Similarly, with Survey Objective 5, you will provide data on the relationship between education and methods of discipline. The difference between stating a survey's purpose as an objective and as a question is a relatively minor change in sentence form from statement to question. Hypothesis testing is a different matter because it requires the rigorous application of the scientific method. **State survey objectives as hypotheses only when you are sure that your research design and data quality justify your doing so.**

For more on hypothesis testing, see **How to Analyze Survey Data** (Vol. 8 in this series).

WHERE DO SURVEY OBJECTIVES ORIGINATE?

The objectives of a survey can come from a defined need. For example, suppose a school district is concerned with finding out the causes of a measurable increase in smoking among students between 12 and 16 years of age. The district calls on the Survey Research Department to design and implement a survey of students. The objective of the survey—to find out why students smoke—is defined for the surveyors and is based on the school district's needs.

The objectives of a survey can also come from reviews of the literature and other surveys. The literature refers to all published and unpublished public reports on a topic. Systematic reviews of the literature tell you what is currently known about a topic; using the available data you can figure out the gaps that need to be filled.

The objectives of a survey can also come from experts. Experts are individuals who are knowledgeable about the survey or will be affected by its outcomes or are influential in implementing its findings. Experts can be surveyed by mail or telephone or brought together in meetings. Two types of meetings that are sometimes used to help surveyors identify objectives, research questions, and research hypotheses are **focus groups** and **consensus panels.** A focus group usually contains up to 10 people. A trained leader conducts a carefully planned discussion in a permissive atmosphere to obtain participants' opinions on a defined area of interest. A consensus panel may contain up to 14 people. The panel should be led by a skilled leader in a highly structured setting. For example, consensus participants may be required to read documents and rate or rank preferences. Example 1.6 illustrates how focus groups and consensus panels can be useful in identifying survey objectives.

EXAMPLE 1.6
Identifying Survey Objectives:
Focus Groups and Consensus Panels

Focus Group

A 10-member group—5 students, 2 parents, and 3 teachers—was asked to help identify the objectives of a survey on teenage smoking. The group met for 2 hours in a classroom at the Middle School. The group was told that the overall goal of the survey was to provide the school district with information on why children start smoking. What information should the survey collect? What types of questions should be on the survey to encourage children to provide honest, and not just acceptable, answers? The focus group recommended a survey that had at least two major objectives:

- Determine the effects of cigarette advertising on smoking behavior
- Compare smoking behavior among children with and without family members who smoke

Consensus Panel

A two-round consensus panel was conducted to help identify the objectives of a survey to find out why children start smoking. The panel consisted of 10 members with expertise in survey research, smoking behavior among children, health professionals, students, and teachers.

In the first round, panelists were provided with a list of potential survey objectives and asked to rate each on two dimensions: their importance and the feasibility of obtaining honest answers to questions pertaining to the objective. The ratings were analyzed to identify objectives that were rated very important *and* definitely feasible. The following table shows a portion of the rating sheet.

Survey Objective	Importance					Feasibility				
	Scale: 5 = Very important; 3 = Somewhat important; 1 = Very unimportant (circle *one* choice for each objective)					Scale: 5 = Definitely feasible; 3 = Somewhat feasible; 1 = Definitely not feasible (circle *one* choice for each objective)				
To determine the effects of cigarette advertising on smoking behavior	5	4	3	2	1	5	4	3	2	1
To compare smoking behavior among children with and without family members who smoke	5	4	3	2	1	5	4	3	2	1

In the second round of the consensus process, panelists met for a half-day and discussed the first round's ratings. After their discussion, the panelists rated the objectives a second time. Objectives were chosen for the survey that at least 8 of the 10 panelists agreed were very important and also definitely feasible.

Straightforward Questions and Responses

Because questions are the focus of many surveys, learning how to ask them in written and spoken form is essential. A straightforward question asks what it needs in an unambiguous way and extracts accurate and consistent information. Straightforward questions are purposeful, use correct grammar and syntax, and call for one thought at a time with mutually exclusive questions.

TYPES OF QUESTIONS

Purposeful questions. Questions are purposeful when the respondent can readily identify the relationship between the intention of the question and the objectives of the survey. A respondent is the person who answers the questions on a survey instrument. Sometimes, the survey instrument writer has to spell out the connection between the question and the survey, as illustrated in Example 1.7.

EXAMPLE 1.7
Purposeful Questions:
The Relationship Between the
Question and the Survey's Objective

Survey Objective: To find out about reading habits in the community

Survey Question: In what year were you born?

Comment: The relationship between the question and the objective is far from clear.

The surveyor should place a statement just before the question that says something like "In this survey of reading habits, we want to be able to compare readers of different ages and backgrounds so that we can better meet the needs of each. The next five questions are about age, education, and living arrangements."

Concrete questions. A concrete question is precise and unambiguous. Adding a dimension of time and defining words can help concretize the question, as shown in Example 1.8.

EXAMPLE 1.8
Concrete Questions

Less Concrete: How would you describe your mood?

More Concrete: In the past 3 weeks, would you say you were generally happy or generally unhappy?

Comment: Adding a time period (3 weeks) and defining mood (generally happy and generally unhappy) adds precision to the question.

Complete sentences. Complete sentences express one entire thought. Look at Example 1.9.

EXAMPLE 1.9
Complete Sentences

Poor: Place of birth?

Comment: Place of birth means different things to different people. I might give the city in which I was born, but you might tell the name of the hospital.

Better: Name the city and state in which you were born.

Make sure that all questions are reviewed by experts and a sample of potential respondents. You should do this even if you are using a survey that someone else has used successfully. The reason is that your respondents may have different reading levels and interests than did users of a previous survey.

Open and closed questions. Questions can take two primary forms. When they require respondents to use their own words, they are called **open.** When the answers or responses are preselected for the respondent, the question is termed **closed.** Both types of questions have advantages and limitations.

An open question is useful when the intricacies of an issue are still unknown, in getting unanticipated answers, and for describing the world as the respondent sees it—rather than as the questioner does. Also, some respondents prefer to state their views in their own words and may resent the questioner's preselected choices. Sometimes, when left to their own devices, respondents provide quotable material. The disadvantage is that unless you are a trained anthropologist or qualitative researcher, responses to open questions are often difficult to compare and interpret. Consider the question in Example 1.10.

EXAMPLE 1.10
Three Possible Answers
to an Open Question

Question: How often during the past week were you bored?
Answer 1: Not often
Answer 2: About 10% of the time
Answer 3: Much less often than the month before

Open questions provide answers that must be catalogued and interpreted. Does 10% of the time (Answer 2) mean not often (Answer 1)? How does Answer 3 compare to the other two?

Some respondents prefer closed questions because they are either unwilling or unable to express themselves while being surveyed. Closed questions are more difficult to write than open ones, however, because the answers or response choices must be known in advance. But the results lend themselves more readily to statistical analysis and interpretation, and this is particularly important in large surveys because of the number of responses and respondents. Also, because the respondent's expectations are more clearly spelled out in closed questions (or the surveyor's interpretations of them), the answers have a better chance of being more reliable or consistent over time. Example 1.11 shows a closed question.

EXAMPLE 1.11
A Closed Question

How often during the past week were you bored? Circle **one.**

Always	1
Very often	2
Fairly often	3
Sometimes	4
Almost never	5
Never	6

TYPES OF RESPONSES

The choices given to respondents for their answers may take three forms. The first is called **nominal** or **categorical.** (The two terms are sometimes used interchangeably.) Categorical or nominal choices have no numerical or preferential values. For example, asking respondents if they are male or female (or female or male) asks them to "name" themselves as belonging to one of two categories: male or female.

The second form of response choice is called **ordinal.** When respondents are asked to rate or order choices, say, from very positive to very negative, they are given ordinal choices. The third form of response choice, **numerical,** asks for numbers such as age (e.g., number of years) or height (e.g., number of meters).

Nominal, ordinal, and numerical response choices are illustrated in Example 1.12.

EXAMPLE 1.12
Three Questions About Movies

1. *Nominal:* Which of these movies have you seen? Please circle yes *or* no for each choice. (The response choices are categorized as yes/no.)

	Yes (1)	No (2)
Gone With the Wind	1	2
Schindler's List	1	2
Casablanca	1	2
Chariots of Fire	1	2
Police Academy 1	1	2
Star Wars	1	2

2. *Ordinal:* How important has each of the following films been in helping form your image of modern life? Please use the following scale to make your rating:

                    1 = Definitely unimportant
                    2 = Probably unimportant
                    3 = Probably important
                    4 = Definitely important
                    9 = No opinion/Don't know

Movie	Please *circle* one for each film				
Gone With the Wind	1	2	3	4	9
Schindler's List	1	2	3	4	9
Casablanca	1	2	3	4	9
Chariots of Fire	1	2	3	4	9
Police Academy 1	1	2	3	4	9
Star Wars	1	2	3	4	9

3. *Numerical:* What is your date of birth?

                    ___ ___ 19 ___
                    Month Day   Year

Each of the questions in Example 1.12 produces different information. The first question asks respondents to tell if they have seen each of six films. The second question asks the respondents to use a continuum to indicate how important each of the six films is to them. This continuum has been divided into four points (with a "no opinion/don't know" option). The third question asks respondents to specify the month, day, and year of their birth.

Survey questions typically use one of three measurement classifications, as illustrated by the three questions in Example 1.12. The first question in Example 1.12, for instance, asks respondents to tell whether or not they fit into one of two categories: saw this movie or did not see this movie. Data or measures like these have no natural numerical values, and they are called nominal or categorical (the names are placed into categories, say, of yes or no). A hypothetical survey finding that uses nominal data results in numbers or percentages, as follows:

> More than 75% of the respondents saw at least one movie or play on the list, but no one saw all six. Of 75 respondents, 46 (61.3%) indicated they had seen *Star Wars*, the most frequently seen movie.

The second measurement pattern, represented by the second question in Example 1.12 is called ordinal. Responses are made to fit on a continuum or scale that is ordered from positive (*very important*) to negative (*very unimportant*). The information from scales like this is called ordinal because an ordered set of answers results. Ordinal data, for example, consist of the numbers and percentages of people who select each point on a scale. In some cases, you may find it expedient to compute the average response: the average rating of importance across all respondents. Sample survey results might take a form like this:

> Of 75 respondents completing this question, 43 (57.3%) rated each movie as definitely or probably important. The average ratings ranged from 3.7 for *Star Wars* to 2.0 for *Police Academy 1*.

Surveys often ask respondents for numerical data. In Example 1.12, respondents are asked for their birth date. From the date, you can calculate each respondent's age. Age is considered a numerical and continuous measure, starting with zero and ending with the age of the oldest person in the survey. When you have numerical data, you can perform many statistical operations. Typical survey findings might appear as follows:

> The average age of the respondents was 43 years. The oldest person was 79, and the youngest was 23. We found no relation between age and ratings of importance.

For more informations on questions, see **How to Ask Survey Questions** (Vol. 2 in this series). Objectives of that volume are the following:

- Understand a survey's cultural, psychological, economic, and political context by:

  - Identifying specific purposes
  - Preparing appropriately worded, meaningful questions for participants
  - Clarifying research and other objectives
  - Determining a feasible number of questions
  - Standardizing the questioner
  - Standardizing the response choices

- Ask valid questions that:

  - Make sense to the respondent
  - Are concrete
  - Use time periods that are related to the importance of the question
  - Use conventional language
  - Use short and long questions appropriately
  - Use loaded words cautiously
  - Avoid biasing words
  - Avoid two-edgers
  - Avoid negative phrasing

- Compare the characteristics and uses of closed and open questions

- Distinguish among response formats that use nominal, ordinal, and numerical measurement

- Identify correctly prepared questions

■ Correctly ask questions by:

- Using response categories that are meaningfully grouped

- Choosing an appropriate type of response option

- Balancing all responses on a scale

- Selecting neutral categories appropriately

- Determining how many points to include on a rating scale

- Deciding on where to place the positive or negative end of the scale

- Determining the proper use of skip patterns

■ Applying special questioning techniques to survey behaviors, knowledge, attitudes, and demographics

2 Sound Survey Design

A design is a way of arranging the environment in which a survey takes place. The environment consists of the individuals or groups of people, places, activities, or objects that are to be surveyed.

Some designs are relatively simple. A fairly uncomplicated survey might consist of a 10-minute interview on Wednesday with a group of 50 children to find out if they enjoyed a given film, and if so, why. This survey provides a description or portrait of one group's opinions at a particular time—a cross section of the group's opinions—and its design is called cross-sectional.

More complicated survey designs use environmental arrangements that are experiments, relying on two or more groups of participants or observations. When the views of randomly constituted groups of 50 children each are compared three times, for example, the survey design is experimental. Definitions of the major survey designs follow.

■ Experimental

Experimental designs are characterized by arranging to compare two or more groups, at least one of which is experimental. The other is a control (or comparison) group. An experimental group is given a new or untested, innovative program, intervention, or treatment. The control is given an alternative (e.g., the traditional program or no program at all). A group is any collective unit. Sometimes, the unit is made up of individuals with a common experience, such as men who have had surgery, children who are in a reading program, or victims of violence. At other times, the unit is naturally occurring: a classroom, business, or hospital.

Concurrent controls in which participants are randomly assigned to groups. **Concurrent** means that each group is assembled at the same time. For example, when 10 of 20 schools are randomly assigned to an experimental group while, at the same time, 10 are assigned to a control, you have a randomized controlled trial or true experiment.

Concurrent controls in which participants are not randomly assigned to groups. These are called nonrandomized controlled trials, quasi-experiments, or nonequivalent controls.

Self-controls. One group is surveyed at two different times. These require premeasures and postmeasures and are called longitudinal or before-after designs.

Historical controls. These make use of data collected for participants in other surveys.

Combinations. These can consist of concurrent controls with or without pre- and postmeasures.

■ Descriptive

Descriptive designs produce information on groups and phenomena that already exist. No new groups are created. Descriptive designs are also called **observational** designs.

Cross sections. These provide descriptive data at one fixed point in time. A survey of American voters' current choices is a cross-sectional survey.

Cohorts. These forward-looking, or **prospective,** designs provide data about changes in a specific population. Suppose a survey of the aspirations of athletes participating in the 1996 Olympics is given in 1996, 2000, and 2004. This is a cohort design, and the cohort is 1996 Olympians.

Cohort designs can also be **retrospective,** or look back over time (a historical cohort) if the events being studied actually occurred before the onset of the survey. For example, suppose a group of persons was diagnosed 10 years ago with Disease X. If you survey their medical records to the present time, you are using a retrospective cohort.

Case controls. These retrospective studies go back in time to help explain a current phenomenon. At least two groups are included. When first you survey the medical records of a sample of smokers and nonsmokers of the same age, health, and socioeconomic status and then compare the findings, you have used a case-control design.

For more information on survey designs, see **How to Design Surveys** (Vol. 5 in this series). Objectives of that volume are the following:

- Describe the major features of high-quality survey systems

- Identify the questions that structure survey designs

- Distinguish between experimental and observational designs

- Explain the characteristics, benefits, and concerns of these designs:

    - Concurrent controls with random assignment

    - Concurrent controls without random assignment

    - Self-controls

    - Historical controls

    - Cross-sectional designs

    - Cohort designs

    - Case-control designs

- Identify the risks to a design's internal validity

- Identify the risks to a design's external validity

Sound Survey Sampling

A sample is a portion or subset of a larger group called a population. Surveys often use samples rather than populations. A good sample is a miniature version of the population—just like it, only smaller. The best sample is **representative,** or a model of the population. A sample is representative of the population if important characteristics (e.g., age, gender, health status) are distributed similarly in both groups. Suppose the population of interest consists of 1,000 people, 50% of whom are male, with 45% over 65 years of age. A representative sample will have fewer people, say, 500, but it must also consist of 50% males, with 45% over age 65.

No sample is perfect. Usually, it has some degree of bias or error. To ensure a sample whose characteristics and degree of representation can be described accurately, you must start with very specific and precise survey objectives. You also must have clear and definite eligibility, apply sampling methods rigorously, justify the sample size, and have an adequate response rate.

ELIGIBILITY CRITERIA

The criteria for inclusion in a survey refer to the characteristics of respondents who are eligible for participation in the survey; the exclusion criteria consist of characteristics that rule out certain people. You apply the inclusion and exclusion criteria to the target population. Once you remove from the target population all those who fail to meet the inclusion criteria and all those who succeed in meeting the exclusion criteria, you are left with a study population consisting of people who are eligible to participate. Consider the illustrations in Example 2.1.

EXAMPLE 2.1
Inclusion and Exclusion Criteria:
Who Is Eligible?

Research Question: How effective is QUITNOW in helping smokers to stop smoking?

Target Population: Smokers

Inclusion Criteria

- Between the ages of 10 and 16 years
- Smoke one or more cigarettes daily
- Have an alveolar breath carbon monoxide determination of more than eight parts per million

Exclusion Criterion: If any of the contraindications for the use of nicotine gum are applicable

Comment: The survey's results will only apply to the respondents who are eligible to participate. If a smoker is under 10 years of age or over 16, then the survey's findings may not apply to these people. Although the target population is smokers, the inclusion and exclusion criteria have defined their own world or study population of "people who smoke."

The survey in Example 2.1 sets boundaries for the respondents who are eligible. In so doing, they are limiting the generalizability of the findings. Why deliberately limit applicability?

A major reason for setting eligibility criteria is that to do otherwise is simply not practical. Including everyone under age 10 and over 16 in the survey of smokers requires additional resources for administering, analyzing, and interpreting data from large numbers of people. Also, very young and older teenage smokers may be different in their needs and motivations. Setting inclusion and exclusion criteria is an efficient way of focusing the survey on only those people from whom you are equipped to get the most accurate information or about whom you want to learn something.

Rigorous Sampling Methods

Sampling methods are usually divided into two types. The first is called probability sampling. Probability sampling provides a statistical basis for saying that a sample is representative of the study or target population.

In probability sampling, every member of the target population has a known, nonzero probability of being included in the sample. Probability sampling implies the use of random selection. Random sampling eliminates subjectivity in choosing a sample. It is a "fair" way of getting a sample.

The second type of sampling is nonprobability sampling. Nonprobability samples are chosen based on judgment regarding the characteristics of the target population and the needs of the survey. With nonprobability sampling, some members of the eligible target population have a chance of being chosen and others do not. By chance, the survey's findings may not be applicable to the target group at all.

PROBABILITY SAMPLING

Simple random sampling. In simple random sampling, every subject or unit has an equal chance of being selected. Members of the target population are selected one at a time and independently. Once they have been selected, they are not eligible for a second chance and are not returned to the pool. Because of this equality of opportunity, random samples are considered relatively unbiased. Typical ways of selecting a simple random sample are using a table of random numbers or a computer-generated list of random numbers and applying it to lists of prospective participants.

The advantage of simple random sampling is that you can get an unbiased sample without much technical difficulty. Unfortunately, random sampling may not pick up all the elements of interest in a population. Suppose you are conducting a survey of patient satisfaction. Consider also that you have evidence from a previous study that older and younger patients usually differ substantially in their satisfaction. If you choose a simple random sample for your new survey, you might not pick up a large enough proportion of younger patients to detect any differences that matter in your particular survey. To be sure that you get adequate proportions of people with certain characteristics, you need stratified random sampling.

Stratified random sampling. A stratified random sample is one in which the population is divided into subgroups or "strata," and a random sample is then selected from each subgroup. For example, suppose you want to find out about the effectiveness of a program in caring for the health of homeless families. You plan to survey a sample of 1,800 of the 3,000 family members who have participated in the program. You also intend to divide the family members into groups according to their general health status (as indicated by scores on a 32-item test) and age. Health status and age are the strata.

How do you decide on subgroups? The strata or subgroups are chosen because evidence is available that they are related to the outcome—in this case, care for health needs of homeless families. The justification for the selection of the strata can come from the literature and expert opinion.

Stratified random sampling is more complicated than simple random sampling. The strata must be identified and justified, and using many subgroups can lead to large, unwieldy, and expensive surveys.

Systematic sampling. Suppose you have a list with the names of 3,000 customers, from which a sample of 500 is to be selected for a marketing survey. Dividing 3,000 by 500 yields 6. That means that 1 of every 6 persons will be in the sample. To systematically sample from the list, a random start is needed. To obtain this, a die can be tossed. Suppose a toss comes up with the number 5. This means the 5th name on the list would be selected first, then the 11th, 17th, 23rd, and so on until 500 names are selected.

To obtain a valid sample, you must obtain a list of all eligible participants or members of the population. This is called the **sampling frame.** Systematic sampling should not be used if repetition is a natural component of the sampling frame. For example, if the frame is a list of names, systematic sampling can result in the loss of names that appear infrequently (e.g., names beginning with X). If the data are arranged by months and the interval is 12, the same months will be selected for each year. Infrequently appearing names and ordered data (January is always Month 1 and December Month 12) prevents each sampling unit (names or months) from having an equal chance of selection. If systematic sampling is used without the guarantee that all units have an equal chance of selection, the resultant sample will not be a probability sample. When the sampling frame has no inherently recurring order, or you can reorder the list or adjust the sampling intervals, systematic sampling resembles simple random sampling.

Cluster sampling. A cluster is a naturally occurring unit (e.g., a school, which has many classrooms, students, and teachers). Other clusters are universities, hospitals, metropolitan statistical areas (MSAs), cities, states, and so on. The clusters are randomly selected, and all members of the selected cluster are included in the sample. For example, suppose that California's counties are trying out a new program to improve emergency care for critically ill and injured children. If you want to use cluster sampling, you can consider each county as a cluster and select and assign counties at random to the new emergency care program or to the traditional one. The programs in the selected counties would then be the focus of the survey.

Cluster sampling is used in large surveys. It differs from stratified sampling in that with cluster sampling you start with a naturally occurring constituency. You then select from among the clusters and either survey all members of the selection or randomly select from among them. The resulting sample may not be representative of areas not covered by the cluster, nor does one cluster necessarily represent another.

NONPROBABILITY SAMPLING

Nonprobability samples do not guarantee that all eligible units have an equal chance of being included in a sample. Their main advantage is that they are relatively convenient, economical, and appropriate for many surveys. Their main disadvantage is that they are vulnerable to selection biases. Two uses of nonprobability sampling are illustrated in Example 2.2.

EXAMPLE 2.2
Sample Reasons for Using
Nonprobability Samples

Surveys of Hard-to-Identify Groups

A survey of the goals and aspirations of members of teenage gangs is conducted. Known gang members are asked to suggest at least three others to be interviewed.

Comment: Implementing a probability sampling method among this population is not practical because of potential difficulties in obtaining cooperation from and completing interviews with all eligible respondents.

Surveys in Pilot Situations

A questionnaire is mailed to 35 nurses who participated in a workshop to learn about the use of a computer in treating nursing home patients with fever. The results of the survey will be used in deciding whether to sponsor a formal trial and evaluation of the workshop with other nurses.

Comment: The purpose of the survey is to decide whether to formally try out and evaluate the workshop. Because the data are to be used as a planning activity and not to disseminate or advocate the workshop, a nonprobability sampling method is appropriate.

The following are three commonly used nonprobability sampling methods.

Convenience sampling. A convenience sample consists of a group of individuals that is ready and available. For example, a survey that relies on people in a shopping mall is using a convenience sample.

Snowball sampling. This type of sampling relies on previously identified members of a group to identify other members of the population. As newly identified members name others, the sample snowballs. This technique is used when a population listing is unavailable and cannot be compiled. For example, surveys of teenage gang members and illegal aliens might be asked to participate in snowball sampling because no membership list is available.

Quota sampling. Quota sampling divides the population being studied into subgroups such as male and female and younger and older. Then you estimate the proportion of people in each subgroup (e.g., younger and older males and younger and older females).

Sample Size

The size of the sample refers to the number of units that needs to be surveyed to get precise and reliable findings. The units can be people (e.g., men and women over and under 45 years of age), places (e.g., counties, hospitals, schools), and things (e.g., medical or school records).

When you increase the sample's size, you increase its cost. Larger samples mean increased costs for data collection (especially for interviews), data processing, and analysis. Moreover, increasing the sample size may divert attention from other sampling activities like following up on eligible people who fail to respond. The diversion may actually increase total sampling error. It is very important to remember that many factors affect the amount of error or chance variation in the sample. Besides nonresponse, these include the design of a sample. If the sample design deviates from simple random sampling, relies on cluster sampling, or does not use probability sampling, then the total error will invariably decrease the quality of the survey's findings. The size of the sample, although a leading contender in the sampling error arena, is just one of several factors to consider in coming up with a "good" sample.

The most appropriate way to produce the right sample size is to use statistical calculations. These can be relatively complex, depending on the needs of the survey. Some surveys have just one sample, and others have several. Like most survey activities, sample size considerations should be placed within a broad context.

Response Rate

All surveys hope for a high response rate. The response rate is the number who respond (numerator) divided by the number of *eligible* respondents (denominator). No single response rate is considered the standard. In some surveys, between 95% and 100% is expected; in others, 70% is adequate. Consider the following two surveys in Example 2.3.

EXAMPLE 2.3
Two Surveys and Response Rates

1. According to statistical calculations, the Domestic Violence Commission needs a sample of 100 for their mailed survey. Based on the results of previous mailings, a refusal rate of 20% to 25% is anticipated. To allow for this possibility, 125 eligible people are sent a survey.

2. A sample of employees at United Airlines participates in an interview regarding their job satisfaction. A 100% response is achieved.

The first survey described in Example 2.3 uses past information to estimate the probable response rate. The survey **oversamples** in the hope that the desired number of respondents will participate. Oversampling can add costs to the survey but is often necessary.

Practically all surveys are accompanied by a loss of information because of **nonresponse.** These nonresponses may introduce error bias into the survey's results because of differences between respondents and others in motivation and other potentially important factors. It is very frustrating and costly to send out a mail survey only to find that half the addressees have moved. As a guide to how much oversampling is necessary, anticipate the proportion of people who, although otherwise apparently eligible, may not turn up in the sample. For mail surveys, this can happen if the addresses are outdated and the mail is undeliverable. With telephone interviews, respondents may not be at home. Sometimes, people cannot be interviewed in person because they suddenly become ill.

Unsolicited surveys receive the lowest fraction of responses. A 20% response for a first mailing is not uncommon. With effort, response rates can be elevated to 70% or even 80%. These efforts include follow-up mailings and use of graphically sophisticated surveys and monetary and gift incentives like pens, books, radios, music and videotapes, and so on.

Nonresponse to an entire survey introduces error or bias. Another type of nonresponse can also introduce bias: item nonresponse, which occurs when respondents or survey administrators do not complete all items on a survey form. This type of bias occurs when respondents do not know the answers to certain questions or refuse to answer them because they believe them to be sensitive, embarrassing, or irrelevant. Interviewers may skip questions or fail to record an answer. In some cases, answers are made but are later rejected because they appear to make no sense. This can happen if the respondent misreads the question or fails to record all the information called for. For example, respondents may leave out their year of birth and just record the month and date.

To promote responses, minimize response bias, and reduce survey error, use these guidelines.

Guidelines for Promoting Responses, Minimizing Response Bias, and Reducing Error

- Use trained interviewers. Set up a quality assurance system for monitoring quality and retraining.

- Identify a larger number of eligible respondents than you need in case you do not get the sample size you need. Be careful to pay attention to the costs.

- Use surveys only when you are fairly certain that respondents are interested in the topic.

- Keep survey responses confidential or anonymous.

- Send reminders to complete mailed surveys and make repeat phone calls.

- Provide gift or cash incentives (and keep in mind the ethical implications of what some people think of as "buying" respondents).

- Be realistic about the eligibility criteria. Anticipate the proportion of respondents who may not be able to participate because of survey circumstances (e.g., incorrect addresses) or by chance (they suddenly become ill).

For more information on sampling, see **How to Sample in Surveys** (Vol. 6 in this series). Objectives of that volume are the following:

■ Distinguish between target populations and samples

    — Identify research questions and survey objectives

    — Specify inclusion and exclusion criteria

    — Choose the appropriate probability and nonprobability sampling methods:

        □ Simple random sampling

        □ Stratified random sampling

        □ Systematic sampling

        □ Cluster sampling

        □ Convenience sampling

        □ Snowball sampling

        □ Quota sampling

        □ Focus groups

■ Understand the logic in estimating standard errors

■ Understand the logic in sample size determinations

■ Understand the sources of error in sampling

■ Calculate the response rate

3 Reliable and Valid Survey Instruments

A reliable survey instrument is consistent; a valid one is accurate. For example, an instrument is reliable if each time you use it (and assuming no intervention), you get the same information. Reliability or the consistency of information can be seriously imperiled by poorly worded and imprecise questions and directions. If an instrument is unreliable, it is also invalid because you cannot have accurate findings with inconsistent data. Valid survey instruments serve the purpose they were intended to and provide correct information. For example, if a survey's aim is to find out about mental health, the results should be consistent with other measures of mental health and inconsistent with measures of mental instability. Valid instruments are always reliable, too.

Four Types of Survey Instruments

Survey instruments take four forms: self-administered questionnaire, interview, structured record review, and structured observation. Each is discussed in turn.

SELF-ADMINISTERED QUESTIONNAIRES

A self-administered questionnaire consists of questions that an individual completes by oneself. Self-administered questionnaires can be mailed or completed "on site," say, on a computer or by hand in a classroom, waiting room, or office. As an example, consider a student who is given a printed form with 25 questions on it about future career plans. The student is told to complete the questionnaire at home and return it to the teacher on Friday. Another type of self-administered questionnaire is the computerized or computer-assisted survey. This type of self-administered survey asks the respondent to give answers to questions directly on the computer. A typical computer-assisted survey presents the questions and the choices on a screen and the respondent uses a keyboard (or voice) to answer the question, as illustrated by this example:

[sample text on screen]

Who is the author of *Macbeth*?
WORDSWORTH
SHAKESPEARE
NOBEL
MACARTHUR

Use up and down arrows to point.
Use space to select
Use left and right arrows to go forward and backward
Hit enter to go to next question
Hit pq to go to previous question

INTERVIEWS

An interview requires at least two people: one to ask the questions (the interviewer) and one to respond (the interviewee). (Group interviews are possible.) Interviews can take place on the telephone, face-to-face, or using television. An example of an interview is when a psychologist directly asks clients to describe their family background and writes the answers on a specially prepared form.

For more about mail, telephone, and in-person surveys, see **How to Conduct Self-Administered and Mail Surveys** and **How to Conduct Surveys by Telephone and in Person** (Vols. 3 and 4, respectively, in this series). Objectives of those volumes are the following:

For Volume 3: **How to Conduct Self-Administered and Mail Surveys**

- Describe the types of self-administered questionnaires

- Identify the advantages and disadvantages of self-administered questionnaires

- Decide whether a self-administered questionnaire is appropriate for your survey question

- Determine the content of the questionnaire

- Develop questions for a "user-friendly" questionnaire

- Pretest, pilot-test, and revise questions

- Format a "user-friendly" questionnaire

- Write advance letters and cover letters that motivate and increase response rate

- Write specifications that describe the reasons for and sources of the questions on the questionnaire and the methodology used in administering the study

- Describe how to develop and produce a sample, identify potential resources for a sample, organize the sample, determine sample sizes, and increase response rate

- Inventory materials and procedures involved in mail and self-administered surveys

- Describe follow-up procedures for nonrespondents, methods of tracking a respondent, and number and timing of follow-up attempts

- Describe how returned questionnaires are processed, edited, and coded

- Describe data entry

- Describe how records are kept

- Estimate the costs of a self-administered or mailed survey

- Estimate personnel needs for a self-administered or mailed survey

- Fully document the development and administration of the questionnaire and the data collected with it

For Volume 4: **How to Conduct Interviews by Telephone and in Person**

- Choose the most appropriate interview mode (telephone or in person) for specific surveys

- Write specific questions with structured interviewer instructions

- Employ appropriate question-writing techniques based on whether the interview will be done by telephone or in person

- Construct useful visual aids

- Organize a flowing interview script that considers possible question order effects

- Write an informative introductory statement

- Write a preletter

- Write a script for a precall

- Design an eligibility screen

- Write and appropriately place transition statements

- Write a job description for an interviewer

- Develop an interviewer training manual

- Design an interviewer training session

- Describe the role of a supervisor

STRUCTURED RECORD REVIEWS

A structured record review is a survey that uses a specially created form to guide the collection of data from financial, medical, school, and other records. An example of a structured record review is the use of a form to collect information from school attendance records on the number and characteristics (e.g., age, reading level) of students who are absent 4 or more weeks each semester.

STRUCTURED OBSERVATIONS

A structured observation collects data visually and is designed to guide the observer in focusing on specific actions or characteristics. For example, two visitors to school would be participating in a structured observation if both are asked to count and record the number of computers they see, look for the presence or absence of air conditioning, and measure the room's area in square feet.

Reliability

A reliable survey instrument is one that is relatively free from "measurement error." Because of this "error," individuals' obtained scores are different from their true scores, which can only be obtained from perfect measures. What causes this error? In some cases, the error results from the measure itself: It may be difficult to understand or poorly administered. For example, a self-administered questionnaire on the value of preventive health care might produce unreliable results if its reading level is too high for the teenaged mothers who are to use it. If the reading level is on target but the directions are unclear, the measure will be unreliable. Of course, the surveyor could simplify the language and clarify the directions and still find measurement error. This is because measurement error can also come directly from the examinees. For example, if teenaged mothers are asked to complete a questionnaire and they are especially anxious or fatigued, their obtained scores could differ from their true scores.

Four kinds of reliability are often discussed: stability, equivalence, homogeneity, and inter- and intrarater reliability.

STABILITY

Stability is sometimes called test-retest reliability. A measure is stable if the correlation between scores from one time to another is high. Suppose a survey of students' attitudes was administered to the same group of students at School A in April and again in October. If the survey was reliable and no special program or intervention was introduced, then, on average, we would expect attitudes to remain the same. The major conceptual difficulty in establishing test-retest reliability is in determining how much time is permissible between the first and second administration. If too much time elapses, external events might influence responses for the second administration; if too little time passes, the respondents may remember and simply repeat their answers from the first administration.

EQUIVALENCE

Equivalence, or alternate-form reliability, refers to the extent to which two items measure the same concepts at the same level of difficulty. Suppose students were asked a question about their views toward technology before participating in a new computer skills class and again 2 months after completing it. Unless the surveyor was certain that the items on the surveys were equal, more favorable views on technology after the second administration could reflect the survey's language level (for example) rather than improved views. Moreover, because this approach to reliability requires two administrations, a problem may arise concerning the appropriate interval between them.

When testing alternate-form reliability, the different forms may be administered at separate time points to the same population. Alternatively, if the sample is large enough, it can be divided in half and each alternate form administered to half the group. This technique, called the split-halves method, is generally accepted as being as good as administering the different forms to the same sample at different time points. When using the split-halves method, you must make sure to select the half-samples randomly.

HOMOGENEITY

Homogeneity refers to the extent to which all the items or questions assess the same skill, characteristic, or quality. Sometimes, this type of reliability is referred to as internal consistency. Cronbach's coefficient alpha, which is basically the average of all the correlations between each item and the total score, is often calculated to determine the extent of homogeneity. For example, suppose a surveyor created a questionnaire to find out about students' satisfaction with Textbook A. An analysis of homogeneity will tell the extent to which all items on the questionnaire focus on satisfaction.

Some variables do not have a single dimension. Student satisfaction, for example, may consist of satisfaction with school in general, their school in particular, teachers, classes, extracurricular activities, and so on. If you are unsure of the number of dimensions expressed in an instrument, a factor analysis can be performed. This statistical procedure identifies "factors" or relationships among the items or questions.

INTER- AND INTRARATER RELIABILITY

Interrater reliability refers to the extent to which two or more individuals agree. Suppose two individuals were sent to a clinic to observe waiting times, the appearance of the waiting and examination rooms, and the general atmosphere. If the observers agreed perfectly on all items, then interrater reliability would be perfect. Interrater reliability is enhanced by training data collectors, providing them with a guide for recording their observations, monitoring the quality of the data collection over time to see that people are not "burning out," and offering a chance to discuss difficult issues or problems. *Intrarater reliability* refers to a single individual's consistency of measurement, and this, too, can be enhanced by training, monitoring, and continuous education.

Validity

Validity refers to the degree to which a survey instrument assesses what it purports to measure. For example, a survey of student attitude toward technological careers would be an invalid measure if the survey only asked about their knowledge of the newest advances in space technology. Similarly, an attitude survey will not be considered valid unless you can prove that people who are identified as having a good attitude on the basis of their responses to the survey are different in some observable way from people who are identified as dissatisfied.

Four types of validity are often discussed: content, face, criterion, and construct.

CONTENT

Content validity refers to the extent to which a measure thoroughly and appropriately assesses the skills or characteristics it is intended to measure. For example, a surveyor who is interested in developing a measure of mental health has to first define the concept ("What is mental health?" "How is health distinguished from disease?") and then write items that adequately contain all aspects of the definition. Because of the complexity of the task, the literature is often consulted either for a model or for a conceptual framework from which a definition can be derived. It is not uncommon in establishing content validity to see a statement like "We used XYZ cognitive theory to select items on mental health, and we adapted the ABC role model paradigm for questions about social relations."

FACE

Face validity refers to how a measure appears on the surface: Does it seem to ask all the needed questions? Does it use the appropriate language and language level to do so? Face validity, unlike content validity, does not rely on established theory for support.

CRITERION

Criterion validity compares responses to future performance or to those obtained from other, more well-established surveys. Criterion validity is made up two subcategories: predictive and concurrent.

- *Predictive validity:* Extent to which a measure forecasts future performance. A graduate school entry examination that predicts who will do well in graduate school has predictive validity.

- *Concurrent validity:* Demonstrated when two assessments agree or a new measure is compared favorably with one that is already considered valid. For example, to establish the concurrent validity of a new survey, the surveyor can either administer the new and validated measure to the same group of respondents and compare the responses or administer the new instrument to the respondents and compare the responses to experts' judgment. A high correlation between the new survey and the criterion means concurrent validity. Establishing concurrent validity is useful when a new measure is created that claims to be better (shorter, cheaper, fairer).

CONSTRUCT

Construct validity is established experimentally to demonstrate that a survey distinguishes between people who do and do not have certain characteristics. For example, a surveyor who claims constructive validity for a measure of satisfaction will have to prove in a scientific manner that satisfied respondents behave differently from dissatisfied respondents.

Construct validity is commonly established in at least two ways:

1. The surveyor hypothesizes that the new measure correlates with one or more measures of a similar characteristic (convergent validity) and does not correlate with measures of dissimilar characteristics (discriminant validity). For example, a surveyor who is validating a new quality-of-life survey might posit that it is highly correlated with another quality-of-life instrument, a measure of functioning, and a measure of health status. At the same time, the surveyor would hypothesize that the new measure does not correlate with selected measures of social desirability (the tendency to answer questions so as to present yourself in a more positive light) and of hostility.

2. The surveyor hypothesizes that the measure can distinguish one group from the other on some important variable. For example, a measure of compassion should be able to demonstrate that people who are high scorers are compassionate but that people who are low scorers are unfeeling. This requires translating a theory of compassionate behavior into measurable terms, identifying people who are compassionate and those who are unfeeling (according to the theory), and proving that the measure consistently and correctly distinguishes between the two groups.

For more information on reliability and validity, see **How to Measure Survey Reliability and Validity** (Vol. 7 in this series). Objectives of that volume are the following:

■ Select and apply reliability criteria, including

  − Stability or test-retest reliability

  − Alternate-form reliability

  − Internal consistency reliability

  − Interobserver reliability

  − Intraobserver reliability

■ Select and apply validity criteria, including

  − Content validity

  − Criterion validity

  − Construct validity

■ Understand the fundamental principles of scaling and scoring

- Create and use a codebook for survey data

- Pilot-test new and established surveys

- Address cross-cultural issues in survey research

Appropriate Survey Analysis

Surveys use conventional statistical and other scholarly methods to analyze findings. Statistics is the mathematics of organizing and interpreting numerical information. The results of statistical analyses are descriptions, relationships, comparisons, and predictions, as shown in Example 3.1.

EXAMPLE 3.1
Statistical Analysis and Survey Data

A survey is given to 160 people to find out about the number and types of movies they see. The survey is analyzed statistically to accomplish the following:

- Describe the backgrounds of the respondents
- Describe the responses to each of the questions
- Determine if a connection exists between the number of movies seen and number of books read during the past year
- Compare the number of books read by men with the number read by women
- Find out if gender, education, or income predicts how frequently the respondents read books

Illustrative results of the above goals of statistical analysis are as follows:

- *Describe respondents' background.* Of the survey's 160 respondents, 77 (48.1%) were men, with 72 of all respondents (48%) earning more than $50,000 per year and having at least two years of college. Of the 150 respondents answering the question, 32 (21.3%) stated that they always or nearly always attended movies to escape daily responsibilities.

- *Describe responses.* Respondents were asked how many movies they see in an average year, and if they preferred action or romance. On average, college graduates saw 10 or more movies, with a range of 2 to 25. The typical college graduate prefers action to romance.

- *Determine relationships between number of books read and movies seen.* Respondents were asked how many books they read in the past year. The number of books they read and the number of movies they saw were then compared. Respondents who read at least five books in the past year saw five or more movies.

- *Comparisons.* The percentage of men and women who saw five or more movies each year was compared, and no differences were found. On average, women's scores on the Value of Film Survey were statistically significantly higher and more positive than men's, but older men's scores were significantly higher than older women's.

- *Predicting frequency.* Education and income were found to be the best predictors of how frequently people go to the movies. Respondents with the most education and income, for example, saw the fewest movies.

In the first set of results, the findings are tallied and reported as percentages. A **tally,** or **frequency count,** is a computation of how many people fit into a category (men or women, under and over 70 years of age, saw five or more movies last year or did not). Tallies and frequencies take the form of numbers and percentages.

In the second set of results, the findings are presented as averages ("on average," "the typical" moviegoer). When you are interested in the center, such as the average, of a distribution of findings, you are concerned with **measures of central tendency. Measures of dispersion,** or spread, like the range, are often given along with measures of central tendency.

In the third set of results, the survey reports on the relationships between number of books read and movies seen. One way of estimating the relationship between two characteristics is through **correlation.**

In the fourth set of results, comparisons are made between men and women. The term **statistical significance** is used to show that the differences between them are statistically meaningful and not due to chance.

In the fifth set of results, survey data are used to "predict" frequent moviegoing. In simpler terms, predicting means answering a question like "Of all the characteristics on which I have survey data (e.g., income, education, types of books read, types of movie seen), which one or ones are linked to frequent moviegoing? For instance, does income make a difference? Education? Income and education?"

What methods should you use to describe, summarize, compare, and predict? Before answering that question, you must answer four others: Do the survey data come from nominal, ordinal, or numerical scales or measures? How many independent and dependent variables are there? What statistical methods are potentially appropriate? Do the survey data fit the requirements of the methods? Nominal, ordinal, and numerical measures have already been discussed, so the next section deals with independent and dependent variables.

INDEPENDENT AND DEPENDENT VARIABLES

A **variable** is a measurable characteristic that varies in the population. Weight is a variable, and all persons weighing 55 kilograms have the same numerical weight. Satisfaction with a product is also a variable. In this case, however, the numerical scale has to be devised and rules created for its interpretation. For example, in Survey A, product satisfaction is measured on a scale from 1 to 100, with 100 representing perfect satisfaction. Survey B, however, measures satisfaction by counting the number of repeat customers. The rule is that at least 15% of all customers must reorder within a year to demonstrate satisfaction.

Your choice of method for analyzing survey data is always dependent on the type of data available to you (nominal, ordinal, or numerical) and on the number of variables involved. Some survey variables are termed **independent,** and some are termed **dependent.**

Independent variables are also called "explanatory" or "predictor" variables because they are used to explain or predict a response, outcome, or result—the dependent variable. The independent and dependent variables can be identified by studying the objectives and target of the survey, as illustrated in Example 3.2.

EXAMPLE 3.2
Targets and Variables

Objective: To compare elementary school students in different grades regarding (a) opinions on the school's new science program and (b) attitudes toward school

Target: Boys and girls in Grades 3 through 6 in five elementary schools

Independent Variables: Gender, grade level, school

Characteristics of Survey: To get gender, ask if male or female; ask students to write in grade level and name of school.

Type of Data: All nominal

Dependent Variables: Opinion of new science program and attitudes toward school

Characteristics of Survey: To get opinions on new science program, ask for ratings of like and dislike (e.g., from *like a lot* to *dislike a lot*); to learn about attitudes, use the Attitude Toward School Rating Scale.

Type of Data: Both ordinal

When choosing an appropriate analysis method, you begin by deciding on the purpose of the analysis and then you determine the number of independent and dependent variables and whether you have nominal, ordinal, or numerical data. When these activities are completed, you can choose an analysis method. Example 3.3 shows how this works.

EXAMPLE 3.3
Choosing an Analysis Method

Survey Objective: To compare boys and girls in terms of whether they do or do not support their school's new dress code

Number of Independent Variables: One (gender)

Type of Data: Nominal (boys, girls)

Number of Dependent Variables: One (support dress code)

Type of Data: Nominal (support or do not support)

Possible Method of Analysis: Logistic regression, a statistical method used when the behavior of interest has two outcomes—support or do not support.

In Example 3.3, the choice of analytic method is labeled "possible." The appropriateness of the choice of a statistical method depends on the extent to which you meet the method's **assumptions** about the characteristics and quality of the data. In the examples above, too little information is given to help you decide on whether the assumptions are met.

For more information on how to analyze data from surveys, see **How to Analyze Survey Data** (Vol. 8 in this series). Objectives of that volume are the following:

■ Learn the use of analytic terms, such as the following:

  – Distribution

  – Critical value

  – Skew

  – Transformation

  – Measures of central tendency

  – Dispersion

  – Variation

  – Statistical significance

  – Practical significance

- *p* value
- Alpha
- Beta
- Linear
- Curvilinear
- Scatterplot
- Null hypothesis

■ List the steps to follow in selecting an appropriate analytic method

■ Distinguish between nominal, ordinal, and numerical scales and data so as to:

- Identify independent and dependent variables

- Distinguish between the appropriate uses of the mean, median, and mode

- Distinguish between the appropriate uses of the range, standard deviation, percentile rank, and interquartile range

- Understand the logic in and uses of correlations and regression

- Learn the steps in conducting and interpreting hypothesis tests

- Compare and contrast hypothesis testing and the use of confidence intervals

- Understand the logic in and uses of the chi-square distribution and test

- Understand the logic in and uses of the *t* test
- Understand the logic in and uses of analysis of variance
- Read and interpret computer output

How to Analyze Data From Open-Ended Questions: One Qualitative Approach

A very common use of a survey is to find out if people are satisfied with a new product, service, or program. Their opinions provide important insights into why new ideas or ways of doing things do or do not get used.

One open-ended set of questions that is particularly appropriate for determining satisfaction requires collecting information about what people like best (LB) about the product or service and what they like least (LL). Here's how the LB/LL method works:

Step 1. Ask respondents to list what is good and what is bad. Always set a limit on the number of responses: "List at least one thing, but no more than three things, you like best about your participation in the focus group." If respondents cannot come up with three responses, they can leave blank spaces or write "none." If they give more than three, you can keep or discard the extras, depending on the information you need.

Instead of asking about the conference as a whole, you may want to focus on some particular aspect: "List at least one thing, but no more than three things, you like best about the instructional materials handed out before the focus group discussion."

Step 2. Once you have all the responses, the next step is to categorize and code them. To do this, you can create categories based on your review of the responses, or you can create categories based on past experience with similar services, products, or activities.

Try to keep the categories as precise as possible—that is, more categories rather than fewer—because it is easier to combine them later if necessary than it is to break them up.

Suppose these were answers that focus group participants gave to the question on what they liked least about the activity:

- Some people did all the talking.
- The leader didn't always listen.
- I couldn't say anything without being interrupted.
- Too much noise and confusion.
- Some members of the group were ignored.
- The leader didn't take control.
- I didn't get a chance to say anything.
- Meles and Petrus were the only ones who talked.
- The leader didn't seem to care.
- I couldn't hear myself think.

You might then categorize and code these answers, as shown in Example 3.4.

EXAMPLE 3.4
Response Categories

Category	Code
Leader didn't listen (ignored participants; didn't seem to care)	1
Some people monopolized discussion (did all the talking; couldn't say anything; Meles and Petrus were the only ones who talked)	2
Disorderly environment (too much noise; leader didn't take control; couldn't hear myself think)	3

Now match your codes and the responses, as shown in Example 3.5.

EXAMPLE 3.5
Group Member Responses

Response	Code
Member A Instructor didn't always listen.	1
I couldn't hear myself think.	3
I couldn't say anything without being interrupted.	2
Member B Leader didn't always listen.	1
Leader didn't take control when things got noisy.	3
The leader ignored some members.	3
Member C I didn't get a chance to say anything.	2

To make sure you assigned the codes correctly, you should establish their reliability. Bring in another rater. Do the two of you agree? In other words, are the ratings reliable? If not, negotiate the differences or redo the codes.

Step 3. When you are satisfied about the reliability, the next step is to count the number of responses for each code. Example 3.6 shows how to do this for 10 focus group participants.

EXAMPLE 3.6
Number of Responses for Each Code

Participant	Codes			
	1	2	3	Total
A	1	1	1	3
B	1	—	2	3
C		2	1	3
D		1	2	3
E		3	—	3
F		2	1	3
G		2	1	3
H		2	1	3
I		3	2	5
J		1	—	1

Look at the number of responses in each category. The 10 focus group members listed 30 things they liked least about the discussion group. Seventeen of the 30 (more than 50%) were assigned to the same category, Code 2, and the surveyor could justly argue that, based on the data, what the participants tended to like least about the focus group was that some people monopolized the discussions and others did not get a chance to say anything.

Next, count the *number* of participants whose answers were assigned to each code—for example, only Participants A and B gave answers that were coded 1 (see Example 3.7).

EXAMPLE 3.7
Participants' Response Pattern

Code	Number of Participants Listing a Response Assigned to This Code	Which Participants?
1	2	A and B
2	9	All but B
3	8	All but E and J

Look at the number of focus group participants whose responses fit each category. Because 8 or 9 of the 10 participants gave responses that fell into the same categories (Codes 2 and 3), their opinions probably represent those of the entire group. It is safe to add that the participants also disliked the disorderly atmosphere that prevailed during the focus groups. They complained that the noise made it hard to think clearly, and the leader did not take control.

When respondents agree with one another, there will be few types of answers, and these will be listed by many people. If respondents disagree, many different kinds of answers will turn up on their lists, and only a few people (fewer than 10%) will be associated with each type.

Interpreting LB/LL data gets more complex when you have many participants and responses to categorize. Suppose, for example, you asked 100 participants to indicate which aspects of a health education program they liked best.

First, you must decide on your response categories and assign each one a code. Then try this:

1. Put the codes in rank order. That is, if the largest number of participants chose responses that are assigned to Code 3, list Code 3 first.

2. Calculate the percentage of students assigned to each code. If 40 of 100 students made responses that were assigned to Code 3, then the calculation would be 40%.

3. Count the number of responses assigned to each code.

4. Calculate the percentage of responses assigned to each code. If 117 responses from a total of 400 were assigned to Code 3, then 29.25%, or *117/400*, of responses were for Code 3.

5. Calculate the cumulative percentage of response by adding the percentages together: 29.25% + 20.25% = 49.50%.

The table in Example 3.8 summarizes these steps with some hypothetical survey data.

EXAMPLE 3.8
Summary of Responses

Response Categories (codes arranged in rank order)	% 100 Participants Assigned to Each Code	No. of 400 Responses Assigned to Each Code	% Respondents Assigned to Each Code	Cumulative % Responses Assigned to Each Code
3	40	117	29.25	29.25
4	34	81	20.25	49.50
7	32	78	19.50	69.00
8	20	35	8.75	77.75
10	17	30	7.50	85.25
1	15	29	7.25	92.50
6	10	14	3.50	96.00
2	5	10	2.50	98.50
9	3	5	1.25	99.75
5	1	1	0.25	100.00

What does this table tell you?

- The highest number and percentages of participants and responses were assigned to Code 3, followed by responses assigned to Code 4.

- Nearly 50% of all responses (49.50%) were assigned Codes 3 and 4.

- Of the 10 coded response categories, more than three fourths (77.75%) were encompassed by 4 codes: 3, 4, 7, and 8.

- Five codes—3, 4, 7, 8, and 10—accounted for nearly all responses (92.50%).

Accurate Survey Reports

Fair and accurate reporting means staying within the boundaries set by the survey's design, sampling methods, data collection quality, and analysis. Accurate survey reports require knowledge of how to use lists, charts, and tables to present data.

LISTS

Lists are used to state survey objectives, methods, and findings. The following illustrations (Example 3.9) of these uses of lists come from a formal talk about a survey of job satisfaction conducted with part-time employees.

EXAMPLE 3.9
Surveys and Lists

1. To State Survey Objectives

   Survey of Part-Time Employees: Purposes

   ### TO FIND OUT ABOUT

   - Quality of life
   - Characteristics of office environment
   - Reasons for part-time employment

2. To Describe Survey Methods

   Seven Tasks

   - Conduct focus groups
   - Identify specific objectives
   - Set inclusion and exclusion criteria
   - Adapt the PARTEE Survey
   - Pilot-test and revise PARTEE
   - Train interviewers
   - Administer the interviews

3. To Report Survey Results or Findings

   PARTEE'S Results

   ### 62% STATE THAT PART-TIME EMPLOYMENT HAS IMPROVED THE QUALITY OF THEIR LIVES.

   - No difference between men and women
   - No difference between younger and older respondents

   ### 32% OF EMPLOYEES ARE ALMOST ALWAYS SATISFIED.

   - Men more satisfied
   - No difference between younger and older respondents

Lists are simple to follow and so are very useful in survey reports.

CHARTS

A figure is a method of presenting data as a diagram or chart. Pie, bar, and line charts are figures. Each has its uses and rules of preparation, as illustrated below. The pie chart shown in Figure 3-1 is used to describe a survey's responses in percentages.

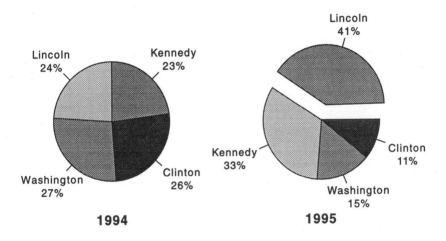

Figure 3-1. Attitude Toward School

As you see, the pie chart is given a title and an explanation of the source of data—telephone interviews. The "slices" show you that the response rates in all four schools were fairly equal proportionately in 1994, ranging from 23% to 27%. In 1995, Lincoln substantially increased its responses, so the range was much wider (from 11% to 41%), and the proportions were less similar among the schools.

Figure 3–2 shows a bar chart. Bar charts (or graphs) depend on a horizontal X-axis and a vertical Y-axis. On the X-axis, you can put nearly all types of data (e.g., names, years, time of day, and age). The X-axis usually has data on the independent variable. The Y-axis represents the unit of measurement, or dependent variable (e.g., dollars, scores, and number of people responding).

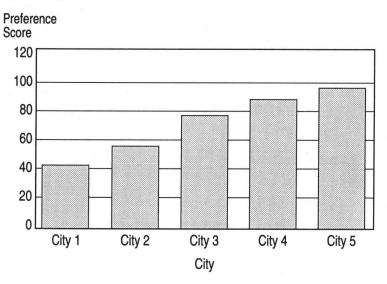

Figure 3–2.   Housing Commission Mail Survey

Bar charts are used in survey reports because they are relatively easy to read and interpret. The bar chart in Figure 3–2 shows the results of a study of housing preferences in five cities. Notice that the chart has a title ("Housing Preferences in Five Cities"), both the X-axis and the Y-axis are labeled (cities and preference score), and the source of data (Housing Commission Mail Survey) is given.

Figure 3–3 shows a line chart in which men's and women's job satisfaction is compared over a 10-year period.

Score

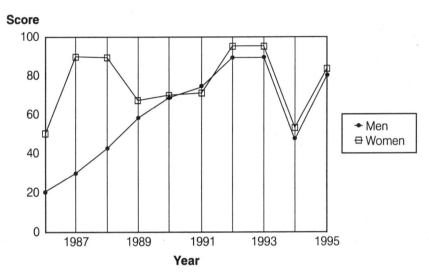

Figure 3–3. Job Satisfaction: A 10-Year Study
SOURCE: The Job Satisfaction Inventory (Higher scores are better)

Because two groups (men and women) are involved in the job satisfaction survey, a key (or legend) to the meaning of the bars is given. The chart shows that men's satisfaction has been lower than women's for 9 of the 10 years. Only in 1991 were the positions reversed and men appeared slightly more satisfied than women.

TABLES

Tables are also frequently used in survey reports. Their major use is to summarize data about respondents and their responses and to compare survey results at one or more times.

Suppose you are responsible for surveying workers in an experiment to find out if their health habits can be improved through an on-the-job health promotion program. One of Company A's two factories is randomly assigned to the experimental program. The other is assigned to the control condition, which consists of free lectures at the company's gym; attendance at the lectures is voluntary. The survey's main objectives are to describe and compare the participants in each program and to compare their health habits (e.g., willingness to exercise regularly) before entering the program, immediately after, and 2 years later. If you achieve the survey's objectives, you will produce tables that look like the empty "shells" in Example 3.10.

EXAMPLE 3.10
Shell Tables to Describe,
Compare, and Illustrate Changes

Description of participants in the experimental and control groups

The table will contain the number (*n*) and percentage of the sample (%) in the experimental group and in the control group of different ages (years), with varying exposures to education, who are male or female, and who speak primarily English, Russian, Spanish, or some other language at home.

	Experimental Group		Control Group	
	n	%	n	%
Age (years)				
Over 55				
45 - 55				
35 - 44				
34 or less				
Education (type of school last attended)				
Graduate school				
College				
High school (or equivalent)				
Gender				
Female				
Male				
Primary language spoken at home				
English				
Russian				
Spanish				
Other (specify)				

Changes over time in the experimental and control groups:
Willingness to exercise regularly

The shell table below is set up to show comparisons among scores on the 25-question Exercise Inventory for the number of people (n) in the experimental group and in the control group.

	Average Scores on Exercise Inventory	
Timing	Experimental Group (n =)	Control Group (n =)
Before program participation		
Immediately after		
2 years after		

When should tables be used? They are especially useful in written reports because they provide detailed information for the reader. Technically oriented people also like them in oral presentations. Unfortunately, little information is available to conclusively guide you in the choice of charts versus tables. If you need to make a visual impact, then charts are appropriate. If you want to illustrate your points with numbers, then tables are appropriate. Often, a mixture of tables and charts is presented in a single report.

For more about survey reports, see **How to Report on Surveys** (Vol. 9 in this series). Objectives of that volume are the following:

- Prepare, interpret, and explain lists, pie charts, and bar and line charts

- Prepare, interpret, and explain tables

- Identify survey report contents for:

  - Oral presentations

  - Written presentations

  - Technical and academic audiences

  - General audiences

- Prepare slides

- Prepare transparencies

- Explain orally the contents and meaning of a slide or transparency

- Explain in writing the contents and meaning of a table or figure

- Explain orally and in writing the survey's objectives, design, sample, psychometric properties, results, and conclusions

- Review reports for readability

- Review reports for comprehensiveness and accuracy

4 Reasonable Resources

A survey's resources are reasonable if they adequately cover the financial costs of and time needed for the survey. This includes the costs of, and time for, hiring and training staff, preparing and validating the survey form, administering the survey, and analyzing, interpreting, and reporting the findings.

How much does it cost to conduct a survey? How can I be sure that I have an adequate amount of resources (time and money) to conduct my survey? These questions are often asked by novice surveyors and experts alike. They can be answered by obtaining the answers to seven other questions:

1. What are the survey's major tasks?

2. What skills are needed to complete each task?

3. How much time do I have to complete the survey?

4. How much time does each task take?

5. Whom can I hire to perform each task?

6. What are the costs of each task?

7. What additional resources are needed?

The meaning of each of these questions and how to answer them are discussed and illustrated in the sections that follow.

What Needs to Be Done?

A survey is a system for collecting information. It often involves deciding on the objectives of the survey, developing a survey instrument, designing a study and identifying the sample, administering the survey, and analyzing and reporting the results. The following is a checklist of typical survey tasks. It may be used as a guide in determining your own survey's tasks. Each of the tasks on the checklist is then explained.

Checklist of Typical Survey Tasks

✓ **Identify the survey's objectives.**

- Conduct focus groups to identify the objectives

- Obtain official approval of the objectives

- Conduct a review of the literature to define terms and justify theory underlying questions

✓ **Design the survey.**

- Choose a survey design (e.g., descriptive or experimental)
- Decide on a sample

✓ **Prepare the survey instrument.**

- Identify existing and appropriate instruments
- Conduct a literature review
- Contact other surveyors
- Adapt some or all questions on existing instruments
- Prepare a new instrument

✓ **Pilot-test the instrument.**

- Identify the sample for the pilot test
- Obtain permission for the pilot test
- Analyze the pilot-test data
- Revise the instrument to make it final

✓ **Administer the survey.**

- Hire staff
- Train staff
- Monitor the quality of administration
- Retrain staff
- Send out mail, supervise the questionnaire, conduct interview
- Follow up

✓ **Organize the data.**

- Code responses
- Consult with programmer
- Train data enterers
- Enter the data into a computer
- Run a preliminary analysis
- Clean the data
- Prepare a codebook

✓ **Analyze the data.**

- Prepare an analysis plan
- Analyze the psychometric properties of instrument
- Analyze the results of the survey

✓ **Report the results.**

- Write the report
- Have the report reviewed
- Modify the report based on the reviews
- Prepare slides, transparencies
- Present the report orally

Getting Each Survey Task Done

IDENTIFICATION OF SURVEY OBJECTIVES

The survey's objectives are its particular purposes or hoped-for outcomes. In general, surveys can be used to describe, compare, or explain knowledge, attitudes, and behavior. For example, a survey can be designed to describe customer satisfaction in Stores A and B, compare satisfaction in A and B, and explain why satisfaction is higher in A than in B.

What are the particular objectives of a survey? For example, in a customer satisfaction survey, should the survey's aim be to compare younger and older persons in their satisfaction? Should information be collected about education or region of the country so that satisfaction can be compared among people with differing levels of education who live in various parts of the country? Methods for answering questions like these include conducting "focus" groups or reviewing the literature.

Once you have identified the survey's objectives, you should certify them "officially." For example, suppose you intend to survey customers and compare men and women of differing educational attainment. Does this meet the needs of the users of the survey? One way to find this out is to create an advisory group of users of the survey. This group may consist of 3 to 5 people who can assist you in keeping the survey on target.

Example 4.1 illustrates how objectives were set for a survey of responses to natural disasters.

EXAMPLE 4.1
Setting Survey Objectives:
What Needs to Be Done?

The Center for Natural Disease Control and Prevention plans to survey victims of floods, fires, earthquakes, and tornados. A mailed questionnaire will be supplemented with interviews. Data from the survey are to be used to determine how to most effectively respond to victims immediately after a natural disaster. What should the survey want to find out? In other words, what should its objectives be?

The survey team first conducts a review of the literature for the definition of the term "victim" and to determine if other surveys of disaster victims are available, and if so, what their objectives are. The team then convenes a six-member focus group that consists of three people who have lived through one or more natural disasters, a psychiatrist whose expertise is in treating people with posttraumatic stress syndrome, and two members of the Agency for Emergency Relief.

Based on the review of the literature and the focus group results, the survey team decides to use a mail survey. The literature reviews and focus groups also result in setting the following four survey objectives:

1. Describe psychological damage associated with the disaster

2. Describe physical damage to person, home, business, school, and so on

3. Identify needs for services during the disaster (for victims of fires and floods)

4. Identify needs for services immediately and 6 months after the disaster

The list of objectives is sent for approval to the Advisory Board, which recommends that Objective 4 be amended to read as follows:

> 4. Identify needs for services within 3 months of the disaster and 12 to 18 months after.

DESIGN OF SURVEY

The objectives of the survey guide the design. For example, if a survey objective is to identify needs for services within 3 months of a natural disaster and 12 to 18 months after, then you know that you must conduct a longitudinal survey or one that collects data over time (in this case, twice: within 3 months of the disaster and then between 12 and 18 months after the disaster). If the objective is to make comparisons, then the survey's design will include two or more groups of respondents.

The next issue that must be resolved is whether you plan to survey everyone or just a sample. If you sample, you must decide on a sampling strategy. Look at Example 4.2.

EXAMPLE 4.2
Survey Design:
What Needs to Be Done?

The Center for Natural Disaster Control and Prevention's survey team decides to conduct a mail survey of a cohort of victims in three states: California, Missouri, and Tennessee. A cohort is a group of respondents that shares an experience (e.g., loss of their home to an earthquake) that is central to the objectives of a survey.

Four cohorts will be surveyed. In California, there will be two: fire victims and earthquake victims; in Missouri, flood victims; and in Tennessee, tornado victims. To find out how many people should be in each cohort, the survey team's statistician conducts a special analysis and finds that at least 50 people are needed in each cohort. Because the study is a longitudinal survey, the statistician recommends having 75 in each cohort, assuming that as many as 25 people may drop out, move, or become inaccessible because of illness or other reasons.

PREPARATION OF SURVEY INSTRUMENT

Once the objectives are set, the survey instrument has to be created. The literature and other surveyors should be consulted to find out if other instruments are available.

If you are lucky, you may find a survey instrument that is designed to collect data that meet the needs of your survey's objectives and that also can be obtained, administered, and scored in a timely and efficient way. You still must check to see that the instrument is appropriate for your population. Is the reading level appropriate? Does the survey ask for all the information you need? Has it been tried out with a population similar to your own? Can you obtain the survey instrument in time? Will you have to pay, and can you afford the price? If you decide to adopt an instrument that is already in use, check the directions to the user and administrator to make sure that they are satisfactory for your purposes.

The most important consideration in adapting a survey instrument is whether it is the type you need. If you want to conduct telephone interviews but the instrument is in the form of a self-administered questionnaire, you must be sure you have the resources to translate it from one type of survey to the other.

If you decide to prepare some or all of your own instrument, you should outline the content, select the response formats (e.g., ratings on a scale from *very positive* to *very negative*) and prepare rules for administration and scoring.

In Example 4.3, a survey team prepares a self-administered questionnaire to find out about people's reactions to natural disasters.

EXAMPLE 4.3
Preparing a Self-Administered Questionnaire: What Needs to Be Done?

The survey team reviews the literature on natural disasters. They focus on reports published by government emergency agencies to identify survey instruments. Twenty appropriate survey instruments are identified: 15 are obtained within the 1-month period allocated for the literature review. None of the surveys is considered wholly appropriate; however, 10 contain at least one question that may be adapted or used in its entirety.

The team prepares an outline of the survey's content and decides to ask questions that have the following format:

Where were you when the earthquake struck? *Please circle ONE response.*

My own home	Yes	No
Someone else's home	Yes	No
Traveling on a city street	Yes	No
Traveling on the freeway	Yes	No
In an office building	Yes	No
In a restaurant	Yes	No
Other (specify)	Yes	No

PILOT-TESTING OF INSTRUMENT

A pilot test is an opportunity to try out an instrument well before it is made final. In a pilot test, you should monitor the ease with which respondents complete the questionnaire and also its ease of administration and scoring.

Usually, you need 10 or more people who are willing to complete the survey. Ask them if they understand the directions for completing the survey and each question and whether the wording in each question and the place to mark responses are clear. Verify the logistics of administering the survey instrument. This is particularly important with interviews. Can interviewers follow the directions that are on the survey form? How long does it take for them to record responses? Do they know what to do with completed interviews? For example, how many should be completed before they are returned to the survey team's office? How many phone calls should be made before giving up on a potential respondent? Use the following questions to guide pilot testing.

Questions to Ask When Pilot-Testing Survey Instruments

Mail and other self-administered questionnaires:

- Are instructions for completing the survey clearly written?
- Are questions easy to understand?
- Do respondents know how to indicate responses (e.g., circle or mark the response; use a special pencil; use the space bar)?
- Are the response choices mutually exclusive?
- Are the response choices exhaustive?

- If a mail questionnaire, do respondents understand what to do with completed questionnaires (e.g., return them by mail in a self-addressed envelope; fax them)?

- If a mail questionnaire, do respondents understand when to return the completed survey?

- If a computer-assisted survey, can respondents correctly use the commands?

- If a computer-assisted survey, do respondents know how to change (or "correct") their answers?

- If an incentive is given for completing the survey, do respondents understand how to obtain it (e.g., it will automatically be sent upon receipt of completed survey; it is included with the questionnaire)?

- Is privacy respected and protected?

- Do respondents have any suggestions regarding the addition or deletion of questions, the clarification of instructions, or improvements in format?

Telephone interviews:

- Do interviewers understand how to ask questions and present options for responses?

- Do interviewers know how to get in-depth information, when appropriate, by probing respondents' brief answers?

- Do interviewers know how to record information?

- Do interviewers know how to keep the interview to the agreed-on time limit?

- Do interviewers know how to return completed interviews?

- Are interviewers able to select the sample using the agreed-on instructions?

- Can interviewers readily use the phone logs to record the number of times and when potential respondents were contacted?

- Do interviewees understand the questions?

- Do interviewees understand how to answer the questions (e.g., pick the top two; rate items according to whether they agree or disagree)?

- Do interviewees agree that privacy has been protected? Respected?

Face-to-face interviews:

- Do interviewers understand how to ask questions and present options for responses?

- Do interviewers know how to get in-depth information, when appropriate, by probing respondents' brief answers?

- Do interviewers know how to record information?

- Do interviewers know how to keep the interview to the agreed-on time limit?

- Do interviewers know how to return completed interviews?

- Do interviewees understand the questions?

- Do interviewees understand how to answer the questions (e.g., pick the top two; rate items according to whether they agree or disagree)?

- Do interviewees agree that privacy has been protected? Respected?

For pilot testing to be effective, you should use respondents who are similar to those who will be asked to participate in the survey. If the survey is targeted to parents of teenaged children, for example, then parents of teenaged children should constitute the pilot test sample.

Use the results of the pilot test to revise the survey instrument and logistics. Sometimes, a pilot test is conducted more than once; this is costly. A field test is a minitrial of the actual survey. For example, a field test of a survey of teenagers' use of health services may take place in one state. The results would then be used to guide any revisions. The final version of the instrument might then be used in a national survey.

ADMINISTRATION OF SURVEY

The survey's administration includes mailing the survey instrument, supervising its use (say, in a classroom), or conducting an interview. To properly administer a telephone survey requires the interviewer to ask questions, record answers, keep records, stay within a time limit, and respect the respondent. To administer a mail survey means packaging the questionnaire (e.g., by including a self-addressed, stamped envelope and ensuring that respondents have enough time to complete all questions), following up with people who do not respond by the due date, and, in some situations, handling rewards and incentives for completed surveys.

A poorly administered survey invariably leads to garbled responses and a poor response rate. To ensure high-quality administration, the staff should be trained and monitored. When hiring staff members, decide on the skills they must have in advance of training. For example, do you want people who can speak a certain language? Who can work between certain hours? Be sure to take the time to train the staff. Have formal training sessions, give each trainee a written manual, and provide practice in conducting interviews. Monitor the results. Observe a sample of interviews, for instance. If they are unsatisfactory, then retrain the interviewers.

ORGANIZATION OF DATA

Organizing survey data means starting with the responses to the survey instrument (the data) and entering them into the computer. To do this, you must assign codes or numbers to all anticipated responses. If the survey instrument is to be completed anonymously or confidentially, you must assign a unique identification number to each respondent. To facilitate direct computer entry, survey questions should be precoded. That is, codes should be assigned to all potential responses before any data are collected. Data enterers should be trained so that data are entered with minimum errors.

ANALYSIS OF DATA

Plan the analysis after you have the survey objectives and know if the data will be nominal, ordinal, or numerical, and if you can explain and justify the quality of the data. Suppose Surveyor 1 wants to compare boys and girls in their willingness to choose future careers in politics. Suppose also that in the analysis willingness is determined by the number of positive answers to a self-administered questionnaire and that a score of 100 is considered twice as good as a score of 50. If the survey data are high quality (e.g., all respondents answer all survey questions on a valid measure) and the data are numerical and continuous, then a t test might be the appropriate analytic method to use to make the comparison. Suppose, however, that Surveyor 2 takes a different approach to analyzing the extent of willingness to choose a career in politics. Surveyor 2 decides that positive willingness is a score of 50 or greater and negative willingness is a score of 49 or less. Assuming the data can be dichotomized, Surveyor 2 might use a chi-square analysis to compare the number of boys and girls with scores of 49 and below and those with scores of 50 and above.

Besides providing survey results (e.g., data on how boys and girls compare in their willingness to choose careers in politics), the analysis can be used to determine the survey instrument's psychometric properties. How do you demonstrate that a score of 100 is twice as good as a score of 50, as posited in Survey 1? To prove that a survey has a scale with equal intervals (e.g., a score of 5 is half the value of a score of 10) requires the kind of analytic proof that psychometricians can provide. Psychometricians are skilled in statistically interpreting a survey's reliability and validity.

REPORT OF RESULTS

Once the data are available, surveyors typically write and disseminate reports or present them orally. In any case, a first draft is rarely acceptable, and reviews and revisions are necessary. In oral reports, slides, overhead transparencies, and other visual aids are often prepared to facilitate the audience's understanding of the survey's message.

Who Will Do It, and
What Resources Are Needed?
Personnel, Time, and Money

A survey happens because one or more persons are responsible for completing the required tasks. In a very small survey, one or two persons may be in charge of planning the survey design, developing the survey instrument, administering it, analyzing the data, and reporting the results. In larger surveys, teams of individuals with differing skills are involved. Sometimes, a survey is planned and conducted by the staff with the assistance of consultants who are called in for advice or to complete very specific activities.

First, you need to plan the activities and tasks that need to be completed. Once this is accomplished, you then decide on the skills required for each task. Next, you decide on the specific personnel or job descriptions that are likely to get you as many of the skills you need as efficiently as possible. For example, suppose your survey design requires someone with experience in training interviewers and writing survey questions. You may just happen to know someone who needs a job and has both skills, but if you do not know the right person, knowing the skills needed will help you target your employment search.

The specific resources needed for each survey will vary according to its size and scope and the number of skills and personnel needed to accomplish each task. Table 4–1 illustrates the types of skills and resources for a "typical" survey. An explanation of the example follows.

Table 4–1
Typical Survey Tasks, Skills, and Resources

Survey Task	Skills Needed	Other Resources
Identify survey objectives	Conduct focus groups	Honorariums for participants Transportation for participants Room rental for meeting Refreshments Materials to guide discussion
	Convene advisors	Honorariums Telephone Mail
	Conduct literature reviews	Librarian Reproduction of materials Standardization of forms for recording contents of literature Computer time for searches Training reviewers

Survey Task	Skills Needed	Other Resources
Design survey	Know alternative research designs and their implementation. Have technical expertise in selecting sampling methods, determining sample size, and selecting sample	Research design expert Computer expert Software Hardware
Prepare survey instrument	Conduct literature reviews Have ability to write questions Have knowledge of the survey's topic Have knowledge of how to assemble questions into an instrument	Same as those needed for survey design Questionnaire expert
Pilot-test survey instrument	Have ability to analyze pilot-test data Have ability to interpret data in order to revise pilot-tested instrument and make it final	Room rental to administer the survey Refreshments for pilot-test sample
Administer survey	*Interviews* Ask questions in standardized, efficient manner Record answers in a standardized, efficient manner Have ability to monitor *Mail* Understand logistics of mailed surveys (e.g., include self-addressed return envelope) Have ability to monitor	Questionnaire expert Training materials expert Expert trainers Room for training Materials for training Materials for retraining Telephones Telephone time Incentives to complete interview Postage Paper Graphics consultant Incentives for completion

→

Survey Task	Skills Needed	Other Resources

Organize data	Code data
	Enter data
	Clean data
	Prepare codebook
		Programmer
		Consultant in data
		  analysis (e.g., what to
		  do with missing data)

Analyze data	Select appropriate data-
	  analytic methods
	Perform data analysis
	Select appropriate
	  psychometric analysis
	Conduct appropriate
	  psychometric analysis
		Programmer
		Statistician
		Software
		Hardware

Report results	Write report
	Prepare slides,
	  transparencies
	Present report
		Duplicating report
		Dissemination (e.g., mail)
		Travel to orally present
		  report
		Honorariums for
		  reviewers
		Editorial consultant
		Slide preparation expert

Survey Tasks, Skills, and Resources: An Explanation

1. *Identify survey objectives.*

A first task requires identifying the survey's objectives. If you use focus groups, you need special expertise in conducting them and interpreting the results. Sometimes, focus group participants are remunerated financially; almost always, they receive refreshments. Other costs that might be incurred are renting a meeting room, transporting the participants, and preparing materials such as literature reviews and survey questionnaires.

A surveyor may decide to use an advisory group to help in obtaining certification of the survey and its objectives. This may require payment of honorariums, transportation to and from a meeting, and the costs of telephone and mail conference calls.

Conducting a literature review as an aid in identifying a survey's objectives requires expertise in identifying relevant sources of information from a variety of places (e.g., the library and public and private agencies), abstracting the information, and displaying the results in a useable fashion. If more than one person is involved in abstracting information, then a standardized form should be prepared so that the same types of information are required from the abstractors; special expertise is needed to prepare abstraction forms. Additionally, the abstractors should be trained by experienced educators to use the form, and the quality of their review should be monitored. Training can take place more than once; depending on the survey, 1 hour or 2 days may be needed. For example, a 2-day training session is not unusual in large surveys of the literature regarding effective social programs and medical treatments.

2. *Design the survey.*

To design a survey requires expertise in research methodologies. For example, research knowledge is essential in deciding on the appropriate intervals in longitudinal studies, determining the inclusion and exclusion criteria for the survey, and for choosing appropriate and meaningful comparison groups.

Sampling is usually considered one of the most technical of all survey tasks because knowledge of statistics is essential in deciding on a sample size, choosing and implementing a sampling technique, and determining the adequacy and representativeness of the sample. Large survey teams include experts in research design and sampling; smaller surveys sometimes rely on expert consultation.

Whenever technical activities take place, it is wise to check on the adequacy of the hard- and software available to the survey team. If it is not appropriate, computers or programs may need to be purchased. In some cases, the existing computer facilities are adequate, but special expertise, like programming, is needed so that the special needs of the survey are met.

3. Prepare the survey instrument.

If the survey instrument is to be adapted from an already existing instrument, expertise is needed in conducting literature reviews to find out if any potentially useful instruments are available. Sometimes, a reasonably good survey is available: Why spend time and money to prepare an instrument if a valid one exists? It helps to have experience in the subject matter being addressed by the survey and to know who is working in the field and might either have instruments or questions or know where and how to get them.

Selecting items or rewording them to fit into a new survey requires special skills. You must be knowledgeable regarding the survey respondents' reading levels and motivations to complete the survey and have experience writing survey questions and placing them in a questionnaire.

Preparing an entirely new instrument is daunting. A job description for an instrument writer would call for excellent writing skills and knowledge of the topic of the survey.

4. Pilot-test the instrument.

Pilot testing means having access to a group of potential respondents that is willing to try out a survey instrument that may be difficult to understand or complete. Expertise is needed in analyzing the data from the pilot test, and experience in interpreting respondents' responses is essential. Additional knowledge is needed in how to feasibly incorporate the findings of the pilot test into a more final version of the survey instrument.

Pilot testing may be very simple, say, a 1-hour tryout by a teacher in the classroom, or very complicated, involving many people, training, room rental, and so on. Also, the survey instrument, even in pilot-test format, must be prepared in a readable, user-friendly format. Assistance with graphics may be useful.

5. *Administer the survey.*

Face-to-face and telephone interviews require skilled personnel. Interviewers must be able to elicit the information called for on the survey instrument and record the answers in the appropriate way. Interviewers must be able to talk to people in a courteous manner and listen carefully. Also, they must talk and listen efficiently. If the interview is to last no longer than 10 minutes, the interviewer must adhere to that schedule. Interviews become increasingly costly and even unreliable when they exceed their planned times.

Mailed questionnaires also require skilled personnel. Among the types of expertise required is the ability to prepare a mailing that is user friendly (e.g., includes a self-addressed envelope) and the skill to monitor returns and conduct follow-ups with those not responding.

Expertise is needed in defining the skills and abilities needed to administer the survey and in selecting people who are likely to succeed. Training is key to getting reliable and valid survey data. For example, a poorly trained telephone interviewer is likely to get fewer responses than a well-trained interviewer. Because of the importance of training, many large surveys use educational experts to assist them in designing instructional materials and programs.

In large and long-term surveys, quality must be monitored regularly. Are interviewers continuing to follow instructions? Who is forgetting to return completed interviews at the conclusion of each 2-day session? If deficiencies in the survey process are noted, then retraining may be necessary.

Telephone interviews, of course, require telephones. Survey centers have phone banks or systems for computer-assisted, random-digit dialing. Face-to-face interviews require space for privacy and quiet. Mailed surveys can consume quantities of postage and paper. All types of surveys may include monetary and other incentives to encourage respondents to answer questions.

6. *Organize the data.*

Organizing the data means programming, coding, and data entry. Programming requires relatively high-level computer skills. Coding can be very complicated, too, especially if response categories are not precoded. Training and computer skills are needed to ensure that data enterers are expert in their tasks. Finally, data cleaning can be a highly skilled task involving decisions regarding what to do about missing data, for example.

7. *Analyze the data.*

Appropriate and justifiable data analysis is dependent on statistical and computer skills. Some surveys are very small and require only the computation of frequencies (number and percentages) or averages. Most, however, require comparisons among groups or predictions and explanations of findings. Furthermore, surveys of attitudes, values, beliefs, and social and psychological functioning also require knowledge of the statistical methods for ascertaining reliability and validity. When data analysis becomes complex, statistical consultation may be advisable.

8. *Report the results.*

Writing the report requires communication skills, including the ability to write and present results in tables and figures. Oral presentations require ability to speak in public and to prepare slides or transparencies. It helps to have outside reviewers critique the report; time must be spent on the critique and any subsequent revisions. Expenses for reports can mount if many are to be printed and disseminated.

TIME, SCOPE, AND QUALITY

Ideally, surveyors prefer to make their own estimates of the amount of time needed to complete the survey. Unfortunately, most surveys have a due date that must be respected.

The amount of time available for the survey is a key factor in the survey's size, scope, and quality and costs. Time limits your hiring choices to people who can complete each task within the allotted time, places boundaries on the survey's design and implementation, may affect the survey's quality, and is a determinant of the survey's costs. Example 4.4 compares two surveys to show the links among time, scope, quality, and costs.

EXAMPLE 4.4
Connections Between Time, Scope, Quality, and Costs in Surveys

Six elementary schools have joined together as a consortium to sponsor a survey to find out why young children start smoking. Among the questions the survey is to answer are these: Do children smoke because their friends do? Do parents smoke and thus serve as a negative model of adult behavior? How influential is advertising? What types of programs, events, or activities are most likely to be effective in teaching young children about the dangers of smoking?

The Consortium Board meets every 6 months. The Board plans to use the survey's results as a basis for determining whether an antismoking program should be undertaken, and if so, what format it might take.

Case Study 1

The Board gives approval for the survey at its September meeting and requires that findings be presented within 6 months in time for its next meeting in March. The survey team's schedule looks like this:

Month 1: Identify objectives and previously used surveys. Conduct a review of the published literature to assist in identifying reasonable aims for the survey. The literature will be used also in helping to locate other surveys that might be appropriate for use in the present survey. (Six months is considered too short a time to develop and properly pilot-test an entirely new instrument.)

Months 1 and 2: Ensure that the sample is readily attainable. The survey team plans to compile a list of families of children in all six schools and make sure that the addresses are current. All children will be included in the survey.

Month 2 and 3: Prepare, pilot-test, and revise the survey.

Month 4: Mail the survey and follow up when necessary.

Month 5: Clean, enter, and analyze the data.

Month 6: Write the report and prepare an oral presentation. .

Comments: The survey team must hire an experienced reviewer because the literature on children and smoking is voluminous; sophisticated skills are necessary to efficiently identify and select the highest-quality, relevant articles and instruments. Skilled literature reviewers cost more to hire than unskilled ones who are trained and supervised. The relatively short time line prevents the team from targeting the survey directly to its own specific population and, with just 1 month for cleaning, entering, and analyzing the data and preparing a written and oral report, requires experienced, skilled (and relatively costly) individuals.

Also, unless items and instruments are available that are demonstrably applicable (e.g., same issues are covered in the appropriate language level), the survey's quality will be compromised.

Case Study 2

The Board gives approval for the survey at its September meeting and requires that findings be presented within 1 year in time for its September meeting. This is what the survey team plans:

Month 1: Identify the survey's objectives. Conduct a literature review and focus groups. Use the focus groups to target the survey's objectives and to determine if the survey should be an interview or a questionnaire.

Month 2: Design the survey. Ensure that the sample list is up-to-date and that all children are included on the list.

Month 3: Prepare the survey instrument.

Month 4: Pilot-test the instrument.

Month 5: Revise the instrument and have it reviewed.

Month 6: Administer the survey and conduct follow-ups.

Month 7: Enter and clean the data, and prepare the codebook.

Month 8: Analyze the data.

Month 9: Write the report.

Month 10: Have the report reviewed.

Month 11: Revise the report.

Month 12: Prepare the final written report and oral presentation.

Comments: The longer time line permits the addition of a focus group for identifying the survey's objectives, a review of the sampling list for accuracy, reviews of the report, and preparation of a codebook.

No guarantees exist that the longer time line will produce a better and more valid survey than the shorter time line. The longer time line is likely to cost more because of the longer length of employment for the team and the additional activities.

SURVEY BUDGETS

How much does a survey cost? This is a two-edged question. A quick answer is that the survey costs exactly the amount of money that has been allocated for it. This can range from $100 to the millions of dollars allocated for the U.S. Census. If you have $5,000 to conduct a survey, well, that is what you have. The only issue is whether you can conduct a survey that you believe will have valid findings, given that amount of money.

Another answer to the question regarding the cost of a survey is related to an ideal or the amount of money and time you need to do a first-rate job. As a surveyor, you are likely to encounter both situations: a. The price is "set," and b. You set the price. Only experience can really tell you if 10 or 15 days is enough to finish task X, and whether person Y is worth the price you are required to pay.

In the next few examples, we assume that when asked to prepare a budget, you are left to your own devices (common enough in government and foundation funding and in business applications, just to name two situations you may encounter). Being left on your own, however, does not mean that a survey can be as expensive as you think you need it to be. On the contrary, everyone loves a bargain. Whatever the cost, you must be prepared to justify your budget, often in written form. Is 10 days enough of Jones's time, for example? Is Jones worth

$5,000 per hour? To justify Jones's time, you will have to demonstrate that he or she is an experienced, even genius, survey developer who is definitely able to complete the task within the time allotted.

How do you calculate the costs of a survey? To answer this question, you must specify all of the survey's activities and tasks, when the activity will be completed, who will be involved in completing each task, how many days each person will spend on each task, the cost-per-hour for each staff person, other direct costs, and indirect costs. Use the following checklist to guide you in calculating costs and preparing survey budgets.

Costs of a Survey: A Checklist

✓ **Learn about direct costs. These are all the expenses you will incur *because* of the survey. These include all salaries and benefits, supplies, travel, equipment, and so on.**

✓ **Decide on the number of days (or hours) that constitute a working year. Commonly used numbers are 230 days (1,840 hours) and 260 days (2,080 hours). You use these numbers to show the proportion of time or "level of effort" given by each staff member.**

   Example: A person who spends 20% time on the project (assuming 260 days per year) is spending .20 × 260, or 52 days or 416 hours.

✓ **Formulate survey tasks or activities in terms of months-to-complete each.**

Example: Prepare survey instrument during Months 5 and 6.

✓ **Estimate the number of days (or hours) you need each person to complete each task.**

Example: Jones, 10 days; Smith, 8 days. If required, convert the days into hours and compute an hourly rate (e.g., Jones: 10 days, or 80 hours).

✓ **Learn each person's daily (and hourly) rate.**

Example: Jones, $320 per day, or $40 per hour; Smith, $200 per day, or $25 per hour.

✓ **Learn the costs of benefits (e.g., vacation, pension, and health)—usually a percentage of salaries. Sometimes, benefits are called labor overhead.**

Example: Benefits are 25% of Jones's salary. For example, the cost of benefits for 10 days of Jones's time is 10 × 320 per day × .25, or $800.

✓ **Learn the costs of other expenses that are incurred specifically for *this* survey.**

Example: One 2-hour focus group with 10 participants costs $650. Each participant gets a $25 honorarium for a total of $250; refreshments cost $50; a focus group expert facilitator costs $300; the materials costs $50 for reproduction, notebooks, name tags, and so on.

✓ Learn the indirect costs, or the costs that are incurred to keep the survey team going. Every individual and institution has indirect costs, sometimes called overhead or general and administrative costs (G and A). Indirect costs are sometimes a prescribed percentage of the total cost of the survey (e.g., 10%).

> *Example:* All routine costs of doing "business," such as workers' compensation and other insurance; attorney's and license fees; lights, rent, and supplies, such as paper and computer disks.

✓ If the survey lasts more than 1 year, build in cost-of-living increases.

✓ In for-profit consultation and contracting, you may be able to include a "fee." The fee is usually a percentage of the entire cost of the project and may range from about 3% to 10%.

✓ Be prepared to justify all costs in writing.

> *Example:* The purchases include $200 for 2,000 labels (2 per student interviewed) @ .10 per label and $486 for one copy of MIRACLE software for the data management program.

The following discussion tells you how to put the checklist into practice.

Direct Costs: Salaries

1. *Determine survey tasks, months to complete, and number of days for each task.*

Suppose the School Consortium (Example 4.4) asks the survey team to plan and prepare a 12-month budget for its Stop Smoking Survey. The team—which consists of Beth Jones, Yuki Smith, and Marvin Lee—begins its budget preparation process by preparing a chart that contains a description of the tasks to be accomplished, the months during which the tasks will be performed and completed, and the number of days the staff will need to complete each task. This is illustrated in Example 4.5.

EXAMPLE 4.5
Tasks, Months, and Staff Days

Task	Month	Staff Members	Number of Days Spent by Each Staff Member on Task	Total Number of Days Needed for All Staff Members to Complete Task
Identify objectives: Conduct literature review	1	Smith	20	35
		Jones	10	
		Lee	5	
Identify objectives: Organize and conduct focus groups	1	Jones	10	15
		Lee	5	

Task	Month	Staff Members	Number of Days Spent by Each Staff Member on Task	Total Number of Days Needed for All Staff Members to Complete Task
Design the survey	2	Lee	15	20
		Smith	5	
Prepare the survey	3	Lee	20	50
		Jones	15	
		Smith	15	
Pilot-test the instrument	4	Lee	15	35
		Smith	10	
		Jones	10	
Revise the instrument	5	Lee	10	15
		Smith	5	
Administer the survey	6	Lee	10	20
		Smith	10	
Enter and clean data; prepare codebook	7	Lee	10	28
		Smith	3	
		Jones	15	
Analyze the data	8	Lee	15	30
		Jones	15	
Write the report	9	Lee	15	25
		Smith	5	
		Jones	5	

$\rightarrow$

Task	Month	Staff Members	Number of Days Spent by Each Staff Member on Task	Total Number of Days Needed for All Staff Members to Complete Task
Have report reviewed	10	Lee	5	5
Revise the report	11	Lee	10	10
Prepare final report and oral presentation Written report	12	Lee	15	35
		Smith	10	
		Jones	10	
Oral presentation	12	Lee	5	15
		Smith	5	
		Jones	5	

This chart enables the survey team to tell how long each task will take and how much staff time will be used. For example, 35 days of staff time is needed to prepare the final report and oral presentation. Soon, the days of staff time will be converted into costs. Obviously, many days of staff time is costlier than fewer days.

Preparing a chart like this is essential. First, it helps you decide where you may need to trim the budget. For example, do Smith and Jones really need to spend 10 days each on the preparation of the final report and oral presentation? What will Lee be doing during the 5 days the report is being reviewed in Month 10? The chart is also useful because it tells you how much time each person is going to be needed for the particular project. For example, Marvin Lee will be working 155 days.

Assuming 260 days is 1 year, Marvin will be spending nearly 60%, or two thirds, of his time on this project. If Marvin also has other projects and very limited time, you may want to ask "Where can we trim Marvin's time and still get the job done?"

Direct Costs: Resources

Practically all surveys require secretarial and clerical support. These persons may also receive benefits if they are employed for a certain percentage of time. (The percentage may vary.) Secretarial and clerical support are sometimes (not always) considered direct costs. You also need to identify any special resources needed for this survey. The following is a potential list of additional resources that are needed for the Stop Smoking Survey to find out about children and smoking.

Task	Special Resources
Review literature	Reproduction of reports and surveys; reproduction of forms for abstracting content of literature
Conduct focus groups	Honorariums for participants; refreshments; notebooks for participants' materials
Design the survey	Honorariums for clerical staff for assistance in reviewing addresses
Prepare the survey instrument	Graphics specialist to help format the questionnaire
Administer the survey	Postage for one original and one follow-up mailing; printing costs for questionnaire
Enter the data	Trained data enterer
Analyze the data	Programmer, statistical consultation
Prepare the report	Paper for multiple copies of the report; graphic specialist for tables
Present the report orally	Program for setting up slides; slide-preparation expert to prepare them for use

Budgets can be prepared for specific activities, individual staff members, and the entire survey. Example 4.6 illustrates the contents that are included in survey budgets. The associated monetary figures are not included because they vary so much from place to place and over time, that information presented at this time may appear ridiculously low (or high) depending on where the survey is conducted and the value of the dollar. Also, Example 4.6 uses a general format for recording budgetary information. If you have all the needed information, you will not have trouble translating from this particular format to another.

EXAMPLE 4.6
Contents of a Budget for
Activities, Staff, and Entire Survey

This is a budget for a 1-year mailed questionnaire.

Budget Contents for an Activity: Present Report Orally

Direct Costs	Cost	Total
Survey personnel		
Marvin Lee—15 days		
Beth Jones—10 days		
Yuki Smith—10 days		
Secretarial support—15 days		
Personnel subtotal		
Benefits (percentage of the subtotal)		
Marvin Lee		
Beth Jones		
Yuki Smith		
Benefits subtotal		

Other direct costs
   Consultant: Slide preparation
   Purchases: MIRACLE software
      Other direct costs subtotal

Indirect costs
   10% of direct costs

      TOTAL BUDGET FOR TASK

Budget Contents for Staff: Marvin Lee

Direct costs
   Days spent on survey: 155
   Salary per day
Indirect costs
   Benefits
      Total for Marvin Lee

Total Budget

   Direct Costs   Cost   Total

   Survey personnel
      Marvin Lee—155 days
      Beth Jones—95 days
      Yuki Smith—88 days
      Secretarial support—165 days
         Personnel subtotal

   Benefits (percentage of the subtotal)
      Marvin Lee
      Beth Jones
      Yuki Smith
         Benefits subtotal

Other direct costs
  Consultants:
    Lanita Chow, Slide preparation
    Graphics artist: To be named
    ABC Data Entry, Inc.
    John Becke, Programmer
    Edward Parker, Statistician
    Purchases: MIRACLE software
    Paper

Other direct costs
  Reproduction of reports, surveys, and forms
  Honorariums
  Postage for survey mailings
  Printing
    Other direct costs subtotal

Indirect costs
  10% of direct costs

    TOTAL BUDGET

BUDGET JUSTIFICATION

Budgets are often accompanied by a justification of any or all of the following: choice of personnel, amount of time they are to spend on a task or on the project, salaries, other direct costs, indirect costs, and any fees or purchases of equipment and supplies. Example 4.7 contains samples of budget justifications for staff, focus groups, and purchase of software.

EXAMPLE 4.7
Budget Justification

Staff

Marvin Lee will be the leader of the survey team and spend 155 days (or 63%) of his professional time on the project. Dr. Lee has conducted local and national surveys, the most recent of which is the Elementary School Behavior Questionnaire (ESB). For the ESB, he successfully performed many of the tasks required in the present study including the conduct of literature reviews and focus groups and survey design, sampling, instrument preparation, data analysis, and report writing. He has worked as a surveyor for this institution for 10 years. His salary is based on his experience and education and is consistent with the salary schedule described in our handbook (which is on file).

Focus Groups

Focus groups are planned to assist in determining the objectives of the survey. We are aiming for 10 participants: 3 children, 2 parents, 2 teachers, 1 health professional, and 2 school administrators. Each will get an honorarium of $XX for a total of $XXX. Each participant will have a specially designed notebook with materials for discussion. Each notebook is $XX to produce, and 10 will cost $XXX. Light refreshments include cookies and soft drinks at $X per person, for a total of $XX.

MIRACLE is a multipurpose graphics program that permits camera-ready slide preparation. Comparison shopping (estimates upon request) found the least expensive price to be $XX.

HOW TO REDUCE COSTS

One of the most difficult aspects of budget preparation is usually performed after the bottom line—the total—is calculated. The reason is that during the first try, we include everything we think we need—and probably then some. Invariably, the budget needs trimming. The following are recommended ways to reduce the costs of a survey.

Guidelines for Reducing Survey Costs

- Shorten the duration of data collection.

- Reduce the number of follow-ups.

- Limit pilot testing to fewer respondents. (If you pilot-test 10 or more in federally funded surveys, you will need to get "clearance" —permission to proceed—from the appropriate federal agency. Nine or fewer in your pilot test also saves time and money.)

- Shorten instrument preparation time by adapting items and ideas from other surveys.

- Keep the instrument brief to reduce interviewer and respondent time.

- Use nonfinancial incentives, such as certificates of appreciation, to reward respondents.

- Use less expensive staff for day-to-day activities.

- Save expensive staff for consultation and leadership.

- Comparison shop for all supplies and equipment.

- Reduce the number of activities.

- Shorten the amount of time each activity takes.

- Use transparencies rather than slides for oral presentations.

Exercises

1. List three sources of survey objectives.

2. Make this question more concrete:

   How would you describe your health?

3. Rewrite these questions so that they are more appropriate for a survey.

   a. Age?

   b. How tall are you?

4. Name the type of sampling used in the following examples:

   Example A: The school has an alphabetical list of 300 students, 60 of which will be asked to participate in a new reading program. The surveyor tosses a die and comes up with the number 3. Starting with the 3rd name on the list and continuing with the 8th, 13th, and so on, she continues sampling until she has 60 names.

Example B: Four of the schools are assigned to the experimental and three to the control group.

Example C: The teachers are asked to give the survey to 10 colleagues.

5. Name four types of survey instruments.

6. Tell whether each of the following statements is true or false.

   a. A reliable survey is one that is relatively free from measurement error.

   b. A reliable survey is nearly always valid.

   c. Test-retest reliability is sometimes called internal consistency reliability.

   d. New Survey A, a measure of self-esteem, has content validity when people who score well on it also score well on Survey B, an older and valid measure of self-esteem.

   e. Construct validity is an appropriate term for a measure of hostility that accurately discriminates between hostile and nonhostile persons.

7. Tell whether each of the following must be considered or can be ignored in choosing a method of analyzing survey data.

	Must be considered (1)	Can be ignored (2)
a. Whether data are nominal, ordinal, or numerical	1	2
b. Reliability of data collection	1	2
c. Validity of data collection	1	2
d. Assumptions of the analysis method	1	2
e. Validity of the research design	1	2
f. Whether the survey is an interview or self-administered questionnaire	1	2

8. What are eight main survey tasks?

9. List 10 questions to ask when pilot-testing mail and other self-administered questionnaires.

10. List 10 questions to ask when pilot-testing telephone interviews.

11. List 8 questions to ask when pilot-testing face-to-face interviews.

Answers

1. The literature, defined needs, and experts

2. In the past month, how often have you felt ill?

3. a. What is your birth date? OR How old were you on your **last** birthday?

   _____ years old

   b. How tall are you in inches?

   _____ inches

4. Example A: Systematic sampling

   Example B: Cluster sampling

   Example C: Snowball sampling

5. a. Interviews (telephone and in person)

   b. Self-administered questionnaires (mail and individual)

   c. Structured observations

   d. Structured record reviews

6. a. true

   b. false

   c. false

   d. false

   e. true

7. a. must be considered

   b. must be considered

   c. must be considered

   d. must be considered

   e. must be considered

   f. can be ignored

8. Identify survey objectives, design the survey, prepare the survey instrument, pilot-test the instrument, administer the survey, organize the data, analyze the data, report the results.

9. *Mail and other self-administered questionnaires*

   1. Are instructions for completing the survey clearly written?

   2. Are questions easy to understand?

   3. Do respondents know how to indicate responses (e.g., circle or mark the response; use a special pencil; use the space bar)?

   4. Are the response choices mutually exclusive?

   5. Are the response choices exhaustive?

   6. If a mail questionnaire, do respondents understand what to do with completed questionnaires (e.g., return them by mail in a self-addressed envelope; fax them)?

   7. If a mail questionnaire, do respondents understand when to return the completed survey?

   8. If a computer-assisted survey, can respondents correctly use the commands?

   9. If a computer-assisted survey, do respondents know how to change (or "correct") their answers?

10. If an incentive is given for completing the survey, do respondents understand how to obtain it (e.g., it will automatically be sent on receipt of completed survey; it is included with the questionnaire)?

11. Is privacy respected and protected?

12. Do respondents have any suggestions regarding the addition or deletion of questions, the clarification of instructions, or improvements in format?

10. *Telephone interviews*

1. Do interviewers understand how to ask questions and present options for responses?

2. Do interviewers know how to get in-depth information, when appropriate, by probing respondents' brief answers?

3. Do interviewers know how to record information?

4. Do interviewers know how to keep the interview to the agreed-on time limit?

5. Do interviewers know how to return completed interviews?

6. Are interviewers able to select the sample using the agreed-on instructions?

7. Can interviewers readily use the phone logs to record the number of times and when potential respondents were contacted?

8. Do interviewees understand the questions?

9. Do interviewees understand how to answer the questions (e.g., pick the top two; rate items according to whether they agree or disagree)?

10. Do interviewees agree that privacy has been protected? Respected?

11. *In-person interviews*

   1. Do interviewers understand how to ask questions and present options for responses?

   2. Do interviewers know how to get in-depth information, when appropriate, by probing respondents' brief answers?

   3. Do interviewers know how to record information?

   4. Do interviewers know how to keep the interview to the agreed-on time limit?

   5. Do interviewers know how to return completed interviews?

   6. Do interviewees understand the questions?

   7. Do interviewees understand how to answer the questions (e.g., pick the top two; rate items according to whether they agree or disagree)?

   8. Do interviewees agree that privacy has been protected? Respected?

Suggested Readings

Afifi, A. A., & Clark, V. (1990). *Computer-aided multivariate analysis.* New York: Van Nostrand Reinhold.

Textbook on multivariate analysis with a practical approach. Discusses data entry, data screening, data reduction, and data analysis. Also explains the options available in different statistical packages.

American Psychological Association. (1985). *Standards for educational and psychological testing.* Washington, DC: Author.

Classic work on reliability and validity and the standards that testers should achieve to ensure accuracy.

Babbie, E. (1990). *Survey research methods.* Belmont, CA: Wadsworth.

Fundamental reference on how to conduct survey research. Good examples of survey questions with accompanying rules for asking questions.

Baker, T. L. (1988). *Doing social research.* New York: McGraw-Hill.

A "how to," with examples.

Bradburn, N. M., & Sudman, S. (1992). The current status of questionnaire design. In P. N. Biemer, R. M. Groves, L. E. Lyberg, N. A. Mathiowetz, & S. Sudman (Eds.), *Measurement errors in surveys.* New York: John Wiley.

Addresses many of the major issues in designing questionnaires and asking questions.

Braitman, L. (1991). Confidence intervals assess both clinical and statistical significance. *Annals of Internal Medicine, 114,* 515-517.

This brief article contains one of the clearest explanations anywhere of the use of confidence intervals and is highly recommended.

Campbell, D. T., & Stanley, J. C. (1963). *Experimental and quasi-experimental designs for research.* Chicago: Rand McNally.

The classic book on differing research designs. "Threats" to internal and external validity are described in detail. Issues pertaining to generalizability and how to get at "truth" are important reading.

Converse, J. (1987). *Survey research in the United States.* Berkeley: University of California Press.

An overview and good examples of how surveys are used in the United States. Helpful in understanding the context of survey research.

Converse, J. M., & Presser, S. (1986). *Survey questions: Handcrafting the standardized questionnaire* (Quantitative Applications in the Social Sciences: A Sage University Papers series, 07-063). Beverly Hills, CA: Sage.

All you need to know on how to put a standardized questionnaire together.

Cook, D. C., & Campbell, D. T. (1979). *Quasi-experimentation: Design and analysis issues for field settings.* Boston: Houghton Mifflin.

Discusses the issues that arise in fieldwork and quasi-experimentation. Helps bring together issues that link design, sampling, and analysis.

Dawson-Saunders, B., & Trapp, R. G. (1990). *Basic and clinical biostatistics.* Englewood Cliffs, NJ: Prentice Hall.

A basic and essential primer on the use of statistics in medicine and medical care settings. Explains study designs, how to summarize and present data, and discusses sampling and the main statistical methods used in analyzing data.

Dillman, D. A. (1978). *Mail and telephone surveys: The total design method.* New York: John Wiley.

The special issues associated with mail and telephone surveys are reviewed.

Fink, A. (1993). *Evaluation fundamentals: Guiding health programs, research, and policy.* Newbury Park, CA: Sage.

Many of the skills needed by survey researchers are shared by program evaluators. Discusses design, sampling, analysis, and reporting.

Fink, A., & Kosecoff, J. (1985). *How to conduct surveys: A step by step guide.* Beverly Hills, CA: Sage.

Gives many examples of survey questions and contains rules and guidelines for asking questions.

Fowler, F. J. (1993). *Survey research methods.* Newbury Park, CA: Sage.

Chapter 6 deals with designing and evaluating survey questions, including defining objectives.

Fowler, F. J., & Mangione, T. W. (1990). *Standardized survey inter-viewing: Minimizing interviewer related error.* Newbury Park, CA: Sage.

Contains good survey question examples and tells how to mini-mize error by standardizing the questioner and the questionnaire.

Frey, J. H. (1989). *Survey research by telephone.* Newbury Park, CA: Sage.

Gives excellent examples of questions and how to get the informa-tion you need from telephone surveys.

Hambleton, R. K., & Zaal, J. N. (Eds.). (1991). *Advances in educa-tional and psychological testing.* Boston: Kluwer Academic.

Important source of information on the concepts of reliability and validity in education and psychology.

Henry, G. T. (1990). *Practical sampling.* Newbury Park, CA: Sage.

Excellent source of information about sampling methods and sam-pling errors. Although statistical knowledge helps, this book is worth reading even if the knowledge is basic.

Kalton, G. (1983). *Introduction to survey sampling.* Beverly Hills, CA: Sage.

Excellent discussion of survey sampling. It requires understanding of statistics.

Kish, L. (1965). *Survey sampling.* New York: John Wiley.

This book is a classic and often consulted in resolving issues that arise when implementing sampling designs.

Kraemer, H. C., & Thiemann, S. (1987). *How many subjects? Statistical power analysis in research.* Newbury Park, CA: Sage.

Complexity of statistical power analysis is thoroughly discussed. Requires an understanding of statistics.

Lavrakas, P. J. (1987). *Telephone survey methods: Sampling, selection, and supervision.* Newbury Park, CA: Sage.

Excellent source of information on all aspects of telephone (and other) survey methods.

McDowell, I., & Newell, C. (1987). *Measuring health: A guide to rating scales and questionnaires.* New York: Oxford University Press.

Provides numerous examples of health measurement techniques and scales available to the survey researcher interested in health. Also discusses the validity and reliability of important health measures.

Miller, D. C. (1991). *Handbook of research design and social measurement.* Newbury Park, CA: Sage.

Discusses and defines all possible components of social research. Part 6 has selected sociometric scales and indexes and is a very good source of questions pertaining to social status, group structure, organizational structure, job satisfaction, community, family and marriage, and attitudes.

Morris, L. L., Fitzgibbon, C. T., & Lindheim, E. (1987). How to measure performance and use tests. In J. L. Herman (Ed.), *Program evaluation kit* (2nd ed.). Newbury Park, CA: Sage.

Excellent discussion of reliability and validity in measuring students' performance.

Norusis, M. J. (1983). *SPSS introductory statistics guide.* Chicago: SPSS, Inc.

This manual accompanies a statistical package for the social sciences. It contains an overview and explanation of the logic behind most of the statistical methods commonly used in the social sciences. The manual also presents and explains statistical output.

Pfeiffer, W. S. (1991). *Technical writing.* New York: Macmillan.

Provides useful tips on the details of putting together formal reports. Discusses the cover and title page, table of contents, and executive summary. Also contains rules for preparing charts and giving oral presentations.

Siegel, S. (1956). *Nonparametric statistics for the behavioral sciences.* New York: McGraw-Hill.

Classic textbook on nonparametric statistics.

Schuman, H., & Presser, S. (1981). *Questions and answers in attitude surveys.* New York: Academic Press.

Raises and addresses many of the important issues in designing questions about attitudes. Contains good examples.

Sudman, S., & Bradburn, N. M. (1982). *Asking questions.* San Francisco: Jossey-Bass.

Very good source for examples of how to write questions pertaining to knowledge, attitudes, behavior, and demographics.

About the Author

ARLENE FINK, PhD, is Professor of Medicine and Public Health at the University of California, Los Angeles. She is on the Research Advisory Board of UCLA's Robert Wood Johnson Clinical Scholars Program, a health research scientist at the Veterans Administration Medical Center in Sepulveda, California, and president of Arlene Fink Associates. She has conducted evaluations throughout the United States and abroad and has trained thousands of health professionals, social scientists, and educators in program evaluation. Her published works include nearly 100 monographs and articles on evaluation methods and research. She is coauthor of *How to Conduct Surveys* and author of *Evaluation Fundamentals: Guiding Health Programs, Research, and Policy* and *Evaluation for Education and Psychology.*